Copyright 2020by Erlene Ramirez- All rights reserved.

This document is geared towards providing exact and reliable information in regards to the topic and issue covered. The publication is sold with the idea that the publisher is not required to render accounting, officially permitted, or otherwise, qualified services. If advice is necessary, legal or professional, a practiced individual in the profession should be ordered.

Under no circumstance will any legal responsibility or blame be held against the publisher for any reparation, damages, or monetary loss due to the information herein, either directly or indirectly.

Legal Notice: The book is copyright protected. This is only for personal use. You cannot amend, distribute, sell, use, quote or paraphrase any part or the content within this book without the consent of the author.

Disclaimer Notice: Please note the information contained within this document is for educational and entertainment purposes only. Every attempt has been made to provide accurate, up to date and reliable complete information. No warranties of any kind are expressed or implied. Readers acknowledge that the author is not engaging in the rendering of legal, financial, medical or professional advice. The content of this book has been derived from various sources. Please consult a licensed professional before attempting any techniques outlined in this book.

TABLE OF CONTENTS

Introduction 6
Breakfast and Brunch 8
    Breakfast Fish Tacos 8
    Shrimp Frittata 9
    Tuna Sandwiches 9
    Tuna and Zucchini Tortillas 10
    Shrimp Croquettes 11
    Shrimp Pancake 12
    Chicken Sandwiches 13
    Cranberry & Cinnamon Oatmeal 14
    Gruyere & Bacon Grits 15
    Honey Stuffed French Toast 16
    Traditional Scotch Eggs 17
    Speedy Pork Roast Sandwich with Slaw 18
    Bell Pepper & Salmon Cakes 19
    Chorizo Cheese Cake 20
Vegetables Recipes 21
    Air-Fried Avocado 21
    Rosemary Potatoes 22
    Falafel Balls 23
    Brussels Sprout Chips 24
    Crispy Potatoes 25
    Honey-Glazed Carrots 26
    Bang Bang Cauliflower 27
    Roasted Carrots 28
    Garlic Rosemary Brussels Sprouts 28
    Air Fryer Chickpeas 29
    Bang Bang Broccoli 29
    Tofu Italian Style 30
    Sweet Potato Tots 31
    Creamy Endives 31
    Zucchini Fries 32
    Balsamic Artichokes 32
    Beet Salad and Parsley Dressing 33
    Broccoli Salad 33

- Brussels Sprouts and Tomatoes Mix 34
- Spicy Cabbage 34
- Collard Greens Mix 35
- Eggplant and Zucchini Mix 35

Fish and Seafood 36
- Tha Fish Cakes With Mango Relish 36
- Air Fryer Fish Tacos 37
- Firecracker Shrimp 38
- Sesame Seeds Coated Fish 39
- Bacon Wrapped Scallops 40
- Crispy Paprika Fish Fillets 41
- Parmesan Shrimp 42
- Flaky Fish Quesadilla 43
- Quick Fried Catfish 44
- Honey Glazed Salmon 45
- Fish and Chips 46
- Fish Sandwiches 47
- Crab Cakes 48
- Crispy Air Fried Sushi Roll 49
- Alaskan Cod with Pinto Beans & Fennel 50
- Scottish Seafood Curry 51
- Meaditerranean Scallops with Butter-Caper Sauce 52
- White Wine Black Mussels 53

Poultry Recipes 54
- Tex-Mex Turkey Burgers 54
- Air Fryer Turkey Breast 55
- Cheese Stuffed Chicken 56
- Orange Curried Chicken Stir-Fry 57
- Mustard Chicken Tenders 58
- Chicken Pot Pie with Coconut Milk 59
- Chicken Nuggets 60
- Cheesy Chicken Fritters 61
- Chicken BBQ with Sweet And Sour Sauce 62
- Crusted Chicken Tenders 63
- Air Fryer Chicken Parmesan 64
- Chicken BBQ Recipe from Peru 65

Ricotta and Parsley Stuffed Turkey Breasts 66
Cheesy Turkey-Rice with Broccoli 67
Jerk Chicken Wings 68
Beef, Lamb and Pork 69
Meatloaf 69
Pork Chops 70
Tender Beef with Sour Cream Sauce 71
Beef Empanadas 72
Beef Pot Pie 73
Bolognaise Sauce 74
Breaded Spam Steaks 75
Air Fryer Burgers 76
Cheese-Stuffed Meatballs 77
Roasted Stuffed Peppers 78
Air Fried Steak Sandwich 79
Carrot and Beef Cocktail Balls 80
Beef Steaks with Beans 81
Air Fryer Beef Steak 82
Mushroom Meatloaf 83
Beef and Broccoli 84
Air Fryer Beef Fajitas 85
Snacks and Appetizer 86
Brussels Sprouts 86
Creamy Potato 87
Green Beans 88
Parmesan Mushrooms 88
Air Fried Eggplant 89
Wrapped in Prosciutto Asparagus with Been Dip 90
Ground Beef & Cabbage Dumplings 91
Paprika Crispy Wings 92
Cheese & Bacon Filled Sweet Potatoes 93
Cheesy Bombs in Bacon 94
Goddess Tomato-Basil Dip 94
Nutty Asparagus 95
Brazilian Snack Pao de Queijo 96
Tomato Bacon Cheeseburger Dip 97

 Cheddar Chicken Dip 98
Desserts 99
 Chocolate Chip Cookie 99
 Marble Cake 100
 Chocolate Cake 101
 Lemon Tarts 101
 Coconut Cookies 102
 Vanilla Cream Cheese Filled Tart 103
 Hot Lava Cake 104
 Christmas Chocolate Cheesecake 105
 Wonderful Vanilla Pudding with Berries 106
 Strawberry Ricotta Cheesecake 107

INTRODUCTION

The Duo Crisp is the latest model of electric pressure cooker made by Instant PoTbsp It is currently only available in the 8- quart size. This two-in-one Instant Pot has two different lids for the two different functions. Use the pressure cooker lid with the pressure cook, saute, steam, slow cook, and sous vide settings. Swap over to the domed air fryer lid to use the air fry, roast, bake, broil, and dehydrate settings.

The Instant Pot Air fryer crisp is revolutionary! It transforms your pressure cooker foods into crispy ones. It also works as a stand-alone air-fryer by roasting, baking, crisping, dehydrating, and air frying any food inside. This Innovative instant air fryer crisp pot ensures tender juicy meals with a crisp, golden finish every time. With this Instant Pot Air Fryer Crisp cookbook, there's much to savor. Move Over French Fries Cook your favorites, indulge in guilty pleasures, and discover new delights you'd never thought to pressure cook and air fry. The Instant Pot Air Fryer Crisp is a fantastic way to cook food that is healthy and easy. It is a fast and safe way of cooking, provides a healthy option, and is easy to clean once it has been used. In this uni q ue Instant Pot Air Fryer Crisp Cookbook, you will find an exclusive collection of recipes to prepare diverse and delicious meals from the comfort of your home. Inside the book, you will find tasty top Instant Pot Air Fryer Recipes under various chapters such as:- Breakfast Recipes-Lunch Recipes- Poultry Recipes- Meat Recipes- Fish and Seafood Recipes- Side Dish Recipes- Snack and Appetizer Recipes Who knew one cooking appliance could do so much so deliciously well? This Instant Pot Air Fryer Crisp Cookbook knows and now you do, too. Get yourself this amazing Instant Pot Air Fryer Crisp recipe book and enjoy cooking now. Enjoy!

BREAKFAST AND BRUNCH

Breakfast Fish Tacos

Cooking Time: 13 minutes
Serves: 4

Ingredients:
- Big tortillas – 4
- Red bell pepper – 1, chopped
- Yellow onion – 1, chopped
- Corn – 1 cup
- Whitefish fillets – 4, skinless, and boneless
- Salsa – ½ cup
- Mixed romaine lettuce, spinach, and radicchio – 1 handful
- Parmesan – 4 tbsps. grated

Directions:
1. Put fish fillets in the air fryer and cook at 350F for 6 minutes. Meanwhile, heat up a pan over medium-high heat; add corn, onion, and bell pepper — Stir-Fry for 2 minutes. On your work surface, arrange tortillas. And build your tacos with all the ingredients. Roll the tacos, place them in the preheated air fryer and cook at 350F for 6 minutes more. Divide fish tacos between plates and serve.

Shrimp Frittata

Cooking Time: 15 minutes	Serves: 4

Ingredients:
- Eggs – 4
- Basil – ½ tsp. dried
- Cooking spray
- Shrimp – ½ cup, cooked, peeled, deveined, and chopped
- Baby spinach – ½ cup, chopped
- Monterey jack cheese – ½ cup, grated
- Salt and black pepper to taste
- Rice – ½ cup, cooked

Directions:
1. In a bowl, mix eggs with basil, pepper, and salt. Whisk well. Grease the air fryer's basket with cooking spray and add shrimp, spinach, and rice. Add egg mix, sprinkle cheese all over and cook in the air fryer at 350F for 10 minutes. Serve.

Tuna Sandwiches

Cooking Time: 5 minutes	Serves: 4

Ingredients:
- Canned tuna – 16 ounces, drained
- Mayonnaise – ¼ cup
- Mustard – 2 tbsps.
- Green onions – 2, chopped
- English muffins – 3, halved
- Butter – 3 tbsps.
- Provolone cheese - 6
- Lemon juice - 1 tbsp.

Directions:
1. In a bowl, mix mayo, tuna, lemon juice, mustard, and green onions. Grease muffin halves with butter. Place them in the preheated air fryer and bake them at 350F for 4 minutes. Add tuna mix on muffin halves, then top each with cheese. Return sandwiches to air fryer and bake 4 minutes more. Serve.

Tuna and Zucchini Tortillas

Cooking Time: 10 minutes
Serves: 4

Ingredients:
- Corn tortillas – 4
- Butter – 4 tbsps. soft
- Canned tuna – 6 ounces, drained
- Zucchini – 1 cup, shredded
- Mayonnaise – 1/3 cup
- Mustard – 2 tbsps.
- Cheddar cheese – 1 cup, grated

Directions:
1. Spread butter on tortillas. Put them in the air fryer basket and cook them at 400F for 3 minutes. Meanwhile, in a bowl, mix tuna with mustard, mayo, and zucchini and stir. Split this mixture on each tortilla, top with cheese and roll tortillas. Cook at 400F for 4 minutes more. Serve.

Tuna and Zucchini Tortillas

Cooking Time: 10 minutes
Serves: 4

Ingredients:
- Corn tortillas – 4
- Butter – 4 tbsps. soft
- Canned tuna – 6 ounces, drained
- Zucchini – 1 cup, shredded
- Mayonnaise – 1/3 cup
- Mustard – 2 tbsps.
- Cheddar cheese – 1 cup, grated

Directions:
1. Spread butter on tortillas. Put them in the air fryer basket and cook them at 400F for 3 minutes. Meanwhile, in a bowl, mix tuna with mustard, mayo, and zucchini and stir. Split this mixture on each tortilla, top with cheese and roll tortillas. Cook at 400F for 4 minutes more. Serve.

Shrimp Frittata

Cooking Time: 15 minutes   Serves: 4

Ingredients:
- Eggs – 4
- Basil – ½ tsp. dried
- Cooking spray
- Shrimp – ½ cup, cooked, peeled, deveined, and chopped
- Baby spinach – ½ cup, chopped
- Monterey jack cheese – ½ cup, grated
- Salt and black pepper to taste
- Rice – ½ cup, cooked

Directions:
1. In a bowl, mix eggs with basil, pepper, and salt. Whisk well. Grease the air fryer's basket with cooking spray and add shrimp, spinach, and rice. Add egg mix, sprinkle cheese all over and cook in the air fryer at 350F for 10 minutes. Serve.

Tuna Sandwiches

Cooking Time: 5 minutes   Serves: 4

Ingredients:
- Canned tuna – 16 ounces, drained
- Mayonnaise – ¼ cup
- Mustard – 2 tbsps.
- Green onions – 2, chopped
- English muffins – 3, halved
- Butter – 3 tbsps.
- Provolone cheese - 6
- Lemon juice - 1 tbsp.

Directions:
1. In a bowl, mix mayo, tuna, lemon juice, mustard, and green onions. Grease muffin halves with butter. Place them in the preheated air fryer and bake them at 350F for 4 minutes. Add tuna mix on muffin halves, then top each with cheese. Return sandwiches to air fryer and bake 4 minutes more. Serve.

Shrimp Croquettes

Cooking Time: 8 minutes
Serves: 4

Ingredients:
- Shrimp – 2/3 pound, cooked, peeled, deveined and chopped
- Bread crumbs – 1 ½ cups
- Egg – 1, whisked
- Lemon juice – 2 tbsps.
- Green onions – 3, chopped
- Basil – ½ tsp. dried
- Salt and black pepper to taste
- Olive oil – 2 tbsps.

Directions:
1. Mix half of the bread crumbs with lemon juice, and egg in a bowl and stir well. Add shrimp, salt, pepper, basil, and green onions. Stir well. In another bowl, mix the rest of the bread crumbs with the oil and toss well. Shape round balls out of the shrimp mix, dredge them in bread crumbs. Place them in the preheated air fryer and cook for 8 minutes, at 400F. Serve.

Shrimp Pancake

Cooking Time: 10 minutes
Serves: 2

Ingredients:
- Butter – 1 tbsp.
- Eggs – 3, whisked
- Flour – ½ cup
- Milk – ½ cup
- Salsa – 1 cup
- Small shrimp – 1 cup, peeled and deveined

Directions:
1. Preheat the air fryer at 400F. Add fryer pan, add 1 tbsp. butter and melt it. Mix eggs with milk and flour in a bowl. Whisk well and pour into the air fryer pan, spread. Cook at 350F for 12 minutes and transfer to a plate. Mix shrimp and salsa in a bowl. Stir and serve pancake with this on the side.

Chicken Sandwiches

Cooking Time: 10 minutes
Serves: 4

Ingredients:
- Chicken breasts – 2, skinless, boneless, and cubed
- Red onion – 1, chopped
- Red bell pepper – 1, sliced
- Italian seasoning – ½ cup
- Thyme – ½ tsp. dried
- Butter lettuce – 2 cups, torn
- Pita pockets – 4
- Cherry tomatoes – 1 cup, halved
- Olive oil – 1 tbsp.

Directions:
1. In the air fryer, mix chicken with oil, Italian seasoning, bell pepper, onion, toss and cook at 380F for 10 minutes. Transfer chicken mixture to a bowl, add cherry tomatoes, butter lettuce, and thyme. Toss well. Stuff pita pockets with this mixture and serve.

Cranberry & Cinnamon Oatmeal

Cooking Time: 10 minutes
Serves: 4

Ingredients
- 2 cups old-fashioned oatmeal
- ¼ cup plain vinegar
- ½ tsp nutmeg powder
- 1 tbsp cinnamon powder
- ½ tsp vanilla extract
- 3¾ cups water
- ½ cup dried cranberries, plus more for garnish
- 2 raspberries, sliced
- ⅛ tsp salt
- Honey, for topping

Directions:
1. Combine the oatmeal, water, vinegar, nutmeg, cinnamon, vanilla, cranberries, and salt in the pot. Seal the pressure lid, choose Pressure cook mode and cook for 10 minutes on High. Press Start.
2. When the timer has ended, perform a natural pressure release for 10 minutes, then carefully open the lid.
3. Stir the oatmeal, drizzle with honey and decorate with raspberries. Serve immediately.

Gruyere & Bacon Grits

Cooking Time: 10 minutes
Serves: 4

Ingredients:
- 3 slices smoked Bacon, diced
- 1 ½ cups grated Gruyere Cheese
- 1 cup ground Grits
- 2 tsp Butter
- Salt and Black Pepper
- ½ cup Water
- ½ cup Milk

Directions:
1. To preheat the cooker, select Sear/Sauté mode and set to HIGH pressure. Cook bacon until crispy, about 5 minutes. Set aside.
2. Add the grits, butter, milk, water, salt, and pepper to the pot and stir using a spoon. Close the pressure lid and secure the pressure valve.
3. Choose the Pressure mode and cook for 3 minutes on High. Press Start.
4. Once the timer has ended, turn the vent handle and do a quick pressure release. Add in cheddar cheese and give the pudding a good stir with the same spoon.
5. Close crisping lid, press BAKE button and cook for 8 minutes on 370 F. Press Start key.
6. When ready, dish the cheesy grits into serving bowls and spoon over the crisped bacon.
7. Serve right away with toasted bread.

Honey Stuffed French Toast

Cooking Time: 25 minutes
Serves: 5

Ingredients:
- 4 eggs
- ¼ cup milk
- 1 tbsp sugar mixed with 1 tsp cinnamon powder
- 6 slices brioche, cubed
- 3 strawberries, sliced, divided
- 2 tbsp brown sugar, divided
- ¼ cup ricotta cheese, at room temperature
- 2 tbsps butter, sliced
- ¼ cup chopped almonds
- 2 tbsps honey

Directions:
8. In a mixing bowl, combine the eggs, milk, and cinnamon sugar, set aside.
9. Grease a baking dish with cooking spray and arrange half the brioche cubes in the dish in a single layer. Lay half the strawberry slices over the bread and dust with 1 tbsp of brown sugar.
10. Spread the ricotta cheese on top of the bread and strawberries. Make another layer of bread, ricotta cheese, strawberries, and brown sugar. Pour the egg mixture over the bread layers ensuring to coat the bread completely.
11. Pour ½ cup water into the pot. Fix the pan on the reversible rack, then put the rack with the pan in the pot. Seal the pressure lid position, choose Pressure and set to High. Set timer to 20 minutes. Choose Start to toast.
12. When done, perform a quick pressure release to let out all the pressure, and carefully open the lid. Top French toast with sliced butter, almonds, and honey.
13. Close the crisping lid. Hit Roast button, and cook for 5 minutes at 390 F. Serve immediately with yogurt and more strawberries.

Traditional Scotch Eggs

Cooking Time: 18 minutes
Serves: 4

Ingredients:
- 1 cup water
- 4 eggs
- 12 ounces Italian sausage patties
- 1 cup panko breadcrumbs
- 2 tbsps melted unsalted butter

Directions:
1. Pour 1 cup of water into the inner pot. Put in the reversible rack place the eggs on the rack. Seal the pressure lid, choose Pressure, set to High, and the Cooking Time to 3 minutes. Press Start.
2. After cooking, perform a quick pressure release, and carefully open the lid.
3. Use tongs to pick up the eggs into an ice bath. Allow cooling for 3 to 4 minutes. Peel the eggs to keep the egg whites intact and blot dry with a clean napkin.
4. Pour the water out of the inner pot and return the pot to the base. Grease the reversible rack with cooking spray and place in the pot.
5. Preheat your cooker by closing the crisping lid; choose Air Fry, set the temperature to 360 F and the timer to 4 minutes. Press Start.
6. Meanwhile, place an egg on each sausage patty. Carefully pull the sausage around the egg and seal the edges.
7. In a bowl, mix breadcrumbs with melted butter. One at a time, dredge sausage-covered eggs in crumbs while pressing into the breadcrumbs for a coat.
8. Open the crisping lid and place the eggs on the rack. Close the crisping lid; choose Air Fry, adjust the temperature to 360 F, and the Cooking Time to 15 minutes. Press Start to start crisping.
9. When the timer has ended, carefully remove the eggs and allow cooling for several minutes. Slice the eggs in half and serve.

Speedy Pork Roast Sandwich with Slaw

Cooking Time: 15 minutes
Serves: 8

Ingredients:
- 2 lb Chuck Roast
- ¼ cup Sugar
- 1 tsp Spanish Paprika
- 1 tsp Garlic Powder
- 1 White Onion, sliced
- 2 cups Beef Broth
- Salt to taste
- 2 tbsp Apple Cider Vinegar

Assembling:
- 4 Buns, halved
- 1 cup White Cheddar Cheese, grated
- 4 tbsp Mayonnaise
- 1 cup Red Cabbage, shredded
- 1 cup White Cabbage, shredded

Directions:
1. Place the pork roast on a clean flat surface and sprinkle with paprika, garlic powder, sugar, and salt. Use your hands to rub the seasoning on the meat.
2. Open the cooker, add beef broth, onions, pork, and apple cider vinegar.
3. Close the lid, secure the pressure valve, and select Pressure mode on High pressure for 12 minutes. Press Start.
4. Once the timer has ended, do a quick pressure release. Remove the roast to a cutting board, and use two forks to shred them. Return to the pot, close the crisping lid, and cook for 3 minutes on Air Fry at 300 F.
5. In the buns, spread the mayo, add the shredded pork, some cooked onions from the pot, and shredded red and white cabbage. Top with the cheese.

Bell Pepper & Salmon Cakes

Cooking Time: 30 minutes
Serves: 4

Ingredients:
- 2 (5 oz) packs Steamed Salmon Flakes
- 1 Red Onion, chopped
- Salt and Black Pepper to taste
- 1 tsp Garlic Powder
- 2 tbsp Olive Oil
- 1 Red Bell Pepper, seeded and chopped
- 4 tbsp Butter, divided
- 3 Eggs, cracked into a bowl
- 1 cup Breadcrumbs
- 4 tbsp Mayonnaise
- 2 tsp Worcestershire Sauce
- ¼ cup chopped Parsley

Directions:
1. Turn on the cooker and select Sear/Sauté on High pressure. Heat oil and add half of the butter. Once it has melted, add the onions and the chopped red bell peppers. Cook for 6 minutes while stirring occasionally. Press Start.
2. In a mixing bowl, add salmon flakes, sautéed red bell pepper and onion, breadcrumbs, eggs, mayonnaise, Worcestershire sauce, garlic powder, salt, pepper, and parsley.
3. Use a spoon to mix well while breaking the salmon into the tiny pieces. Use your hands to mold 4 patties out of the mixture.
4. Add the remaining butter to melt, and when melted, add the patties. Fry for 4 minutes, flipping once.
5. Close the crisping lid, select Bake mode and bake for 4 minutes on 320 F. Remove them onto a wire rack to rest. Serve.

Chorizo Cheese Cake

Cooking Time: 10 minutes
Serves: 6

Ingredients:
- 8 Eggs, cracked into a bowl
- 8 oz Chorizo Sausage, chopped
- 3 Bacon Slices, chopped
- 1 large Green Bell Pepper, chopped
- 1 large Red Bell Pepper, chopped
- 1 cup chopped Green Onion
- 1 cup grated Cheddar Cheese
- 1 tsp Red Chili Flakes
- Salt and Black Pepper to taste
- ½ cup Milk
- 4 slices Bread, cut into ½ -inch cubes

Directions:
1. Add the eggs, sausage chorizo, bacon slices, green and red bell peppers, green onion, chili flakes, cheddar cheese, salt, pepper, and milk to a bowl and use a whisk to beat them together.
2. Grease a bundt pan with cooking spray and pour the egg mixture into it. After, drop the bread slices in the egg mixture all around while using a spoon to push them into the mixture.
3. Open the cooker, pour in 2 cups water, and fit the rack at the center of the pot. Place bundt pan on the rack and seal the pressure lid. Select Pressure mode on High pressure for 6 minutes, and press Start.
4. Once the timer goes off, press Cancel, do a quick pressure release. Run a knife around the egg in the bundt pan, close the crisping lid and cook for another 4 minutes on Bake on 380 F. When ready, place a serving plate on the bundt pan, and then, turn the egg bundt over. Cut the egg into slices. Serve.

VEGETABLES RECIPES

Air-Fried Avocado

Cooking Time: 6 minutes
Serves: 2

Ingredients:
- All-purpose flour – ½ cup
- Avocados – 2, cut into wedges
- Eggs – 2
- Mayonnaise – 2 tbsps.
- Apple cider vinegar – 1 tbsp.
- Sriracha chili sauce – 1 tbsp.
- Black pepper – ½ tsps.
- Kosher salt – ¼ tsp.
- Panko breadcrumbs – ½ cup
- No-salt-added ketchup – ¼ cup
- Water – 1 tbsp.
- Cooking spray

Directions:
1. Arrange three bowls. Add flour, and pepper in the first bowl, beaten eggs in the second bowl, and breadcrumbs in a third bowl. Dredge avocado wedges in the flour, then egg and dip in the breadcrumbs. Coat well and spray with cooking oil. Bake in the air fryer at 400F for 4 minutes. Then flip the avocados and cook for 2 minutes more. Remove and season with salt. Mix the remaining ingredients to make a sauce. Serve.

Rosemary Potatoes

Cooking Time: 15 minutes
Serves: 2

Ingredients:
- Vegetable oil – 3 tbsps.
- Yellow baby potatoes – 4, quartered
- Dried rosemary minced – 2 tsps.
- Minced garlic – 1 tbsp.
- Ground black pepper – 1 tsp.
- Chopped parsley – ¼ cup
- Fresh lime juice – 1 tbsp.
- Salt -1 tsp.

Directions:
1. In a bowl, add potatoes, garlic, rosemary, pepper, and salt. Mix well. Bake in the air fryer at 400F for 15 minutes. Flip the potatoes at the halfway mark. Then sprinkle with lemon juice and parsley and serve.

Falafel Balls

Cooking Time: 12 minutes
Serves: 3

Ingredients:
- Sweet onion – ½ cup, diced
- Oil – 2 tbsps.
- Turmeric – ½ tsp.
- Carrots – ½ cup, minced
- Rolled oats -1 cup
- Roasted, salted cashews – ½ cup
- Cooked chickpeas – 2 cups, drained and rinsed
- Juice of 1 lemon
- Soy sauce – 2 tbsps.
- Flax meal – 1 tbsp.
- Garlic powder – ½ tsp.
- Ground cumin – ½

Directions:
1. Heat a little oil and sauté onions and carrots in the Instant Pot Duo. Cook for 7 minutes, then transfer to a bowl. Place cashew and oats in a food processor and process until you get a coarse meal consistency. Add this mixture to the bowl with vegetables. Place the chickpeas, lemon juice and soy sauce into the food processor and puree until a semi-smooth consistency. Transfer it to the bowl and add in the flax and spices. Mix well. Form falafel balls. Line the air fryer with parchment paper. Cook the balls in the air fryer at 370F for 12 minutes. Shake the basket after 8 minutes of cooking. Serve.

Brussels Sprout Chips

Cooking Time: 8 minutes
Serves: 3

Ingredients:
- Brussels sprouts – ½ pound, sliced
- Garlic powder - 1 tsp.
- Olive oil – 1 tbsp.
- Parmesan – 2 tbsps. plus 2 tbsps. shredded
- Ground black pepper and salt to taste
- Caesar dressing – ¼ cup for dipping

Directions:
1. Toss 2 tbsps. Parmesan, sliced Brussels, and garlic powder in a bowl. Season with salt and pepper. Bake in the air fryer at 350F for 8 minutes. Shake at the halfway mark. Then remove and garnish with parmesan. Serve with Caesar dressing.

Crispy Potatoes

Cooking Time: 18 minutes
Serves: 4

Ingredients:
- Baby potatoes – 1 pound, chopped with peel
- Oil – 1 tbsp.
- Italian seasoning – 1 tsp.
- Garlic powder – 1 tsp.
- Cajun seasoning – 1 tsp.
- Salt and pepper to taste
- Lemons – 2, cut into wedges
- Chopped parsley – ¼ cup, for garnish

Directions:
1. Toss garlic powder, halved potatoes, Cajun seasoning, Italian seasoning, salt in a bowl and mix with potatoes. Bake in the air fryer at 400F for 18 minutes. Shake the potatoes after 10 minutes of cooking. Finish cooking and serve with lemon wedges and parsley.

Honey-Glazed Carrots

Cooking Time: 35 minutes
Serves: 6

Ingredients:
- Carrots – 2 pounds, peeled and cut lengthwise
- Honey – 2 tbsps.
- Butter – ¼ cup
- Garlic powder – ½ tsp.
- Rosemary – ½ tsp. dried
- Salt and pepper to taste
- Fresh thyme – 4 tbsps. chopped

Directions:
1. Melt butter in a saucepan. Add garlic powder, rosemary, honey, pepper, and salt and mix well. Remove and set aside. Add the carrots and mix. Preheat the air fryer at 400F. Line the air fryer basket with a baking sheet and cook the carrots at 400F for 35 minutes. Garnish and serve.

Bang Bang Cauliflower

Cooking Time: 12 minutes
Serves: 4

Ingredients:
- Cauliflower – 21 ounces, chopped
- Olive oil – 3 tbsps.
- Garlic – 3 cloves, grated
- Lime zest of 1 lime
- Sriracha – 1 tbsp.
- Sweet chili sauce - 2 tbsps.
- Salt and pepper to taste
- Chopped cilantro – 1 tsp. for garnish

Directions:
1. Combine oil, chili sauce, lime juice, sriracha, and garlic in a bowl. Add the cauliflower, ground pepper, salt and mix. Cook in the air fryer at 360F for 12 minutes. Shake the basket at the halfway mark. Garnish and serve.

Roasted Carrots

Cooking Time: 30 minutes
Serves: 4

Ingredients:
- Carrots – 2 pounds, quartered
- Olive oil – 3 tbsps.
- Black pepper and salt to taste
- Chopped parsley – ¼ cup, fresh for garnish

Directions:
1. Combine everything in a bowl, except for the parsley. Mix well. Cook in the air fryer at 400F for 30 minutes. Shake the basket at the halfway mark. Serve with chopped parsley.

Garlic Rosemary Brussels Sprouts

Cooking Time: 13 minutes   Serves: 4

Ingredients:
- Brussels sprouts – 1 pound, halved
- Olive oil - 3 tbsps.
- Panko breadcrumbs – ½ cup
- Garlic – 2 cloves, chopped
- Salt and pepper to taste
- Chopped fresh rosemary -1 ½ tsps.

Directions:
1. In a bowl, put pepper, salt, garlic, and oil and microwave for 30 seconds. Preheat the air fryer for 5 minutes at 350F. Mix the Brussels sprouts in the heated oil mixture. Cook in the air fryer for 8 minutes. Shake the basket after 5 minutes and then finish cooking. In a bowl combine breadcrumbs, remaining oil mixture and rosemary. When the cooking is over, open the air fryer and sprinkle the breadcrumb mixture over the sprouts. Close and cook for 5 minutes more. Serve.

Air Fryer Chickpeas

Cooking Time: 20 minutes   Serves: 4

Ingredients:
- Canned chickpeas – 15 ½ ounces, rinsed and drained
- Cumin powder – ¼ tsp.
- Cayenne pepper powder – ¼ tsp.
- Salt – 1 tsp.
- Cooking spray

Directions:
1. Cook the chickpeas in the air fryer at 390F for 20 minutes. Meantime, combine cumin powder, cayenne pepper, and salt in a bowl. After 5 minutes, open the lid and spray some oil on the chickpeas. Sprinkle a quarter of the seasoning and stir the chickpeas with a spoon. Close and continue to cook. Shake the basket after every 5 minutes. Remove from the air fryer and add the remaining seasoning. Mix and serve.

Bang Bang Broccoli

Cooking Time: 20 minutes
Serves: 4

Ingredients:
- Broccoli – 2 pounds, chopped
- Extra-virgin olive oil – 3 tbsps.
- Sriracha – 1 tbsp.
- Sweet chili sauce – 2 tbsps.
- Lime zest – 1
- Salt and pepper to taste

Directions:
1. Preheat the air fryer at 425F for 5 minutes. Whisk sriracha, chili sauce, lime zest, and oil in a bowl. Mix the broccoli with the sauce. Add salt and pepper and mix again. Cook in the air fryer for 20 minutes. Shake once. Serve.

Tofu Italian Style

Cooking Time: 10 minutes
Serves: 2

Ingredients:
- Tofu – 8 ounces, extra-firm, drained, sliced lengthwise and excess water removed
- Broth – 1 tbsp.
- Soy sauce – 1 tbsp.
- Basil – ½ tsp. dried
- Oregano – ½ tsp. dried
- Onion powder – ½ tsp.
- Garlic powder – ½ tsp.
- Black pepper and salt to taste

Directions:
1. Slice the tofu into cubes and put in a Ziplock bag. Mix all the ingredients in a bowl. Add this mixture to the Ziplock bag and mix well. Preheat the air fryer at 400F for 5 minutes. Add the seasoned tofu in the air fryer and cook at 350F for 6 minutes. Open the air fryer after 4 minutes and shake the basket. Finish cooking. Serve.

Sweet Potato Tots

Cooking Time: 14 minutes   Serves: 4

Ingredients:
- Sweet potatoes – 14 ounces, peeled and washed
- Potato starch – 1 tbsp.
- Garlic powder – 1/8 tsp.
- Salt to taste
- Saltless ketchup – ¾ cup
- Oil for cooking

Directions:
1. Boil the sweet potatoes for 15 minutes until they become tender. Then cool, and shred the sweet potatoes. Add salt, garlic powder, and potato starch. Make 24 tots from this mixture. Grease the air fryer basket with oil. Place the tots in the basket and spray with cooking spray. Cook at 400F for 14 minutes. Shake the basket at the halfway mark. Serve with ketchup.

Creamy Endives

Cooking Time: 10 minutes   Serves: 6

Ingredients:
- Endives – 6, trimmed and halved
- Garlic powder – 1 tsp.
- Greek yogurt – ½ cup
- Curry powder – ½ tsp.
- Salt and black pepper to taste
- Lemon juice – 3 tbsps.

Directions:
1. In a bowl, mix endives with lemon juice, salt, pepper, curry powder, yogurt, and garlic powder. Coat well and set aside for 10 minutes. Cook in the preheated 350F air fryer for 10 minutes. Serve.

Zucchini Fries

Cooking Time: 12 minutes   Serves: 4

Ingredients:
- Zucchini – 1, cut into medium sticks
- Olive oil – 1 drizzle
- Salt and black pepper to taste
- Eggs – 2, whisked
- Bread crumbs – 1 cup
- Flour – ½ cup

Directions:
1. In a bowl, add flour and mix with salt and pepper. Put breadcrumbs in another bowl. In a third bowl, mix the egg with salt and pepper. Dredge zucchini fries in flour, then in eggs and in bread crumbs. Grease the air fryer with olive oil. Heat up at 400F. Add zucchini fries and cook them for 12 minutes. Serve.

Balsamic Artichokes

Cooking Time: 7 minutes   Serves: 4

Ingredients:
- Big artichokes – 4, trimmed
- Salt and black pepper to taste
- Lemon juice – 2 tbsps.
- Extra-virgin olive oil – ¼ cup
- Garlic – 2 cloves, minced
- Balsamic vinegar – 2 tsps.
- Oregano – 1 tsp. dried

Directions:
1. Season artichokes with salt and pepper. Rub with half of the lemon juice and half of the oil. Cook in the air fryer at 360F for 7 minutes. Meanwhile, in a bowl, mix the remaining oil, and lemon juice with vinegar, salt, pepper, garlic, and oregano. Mix well. Arrange artichokes on a platter. Drizzle the balsamic vinaigrette over them and serve.

Beet Salad and Parsley Dressing

Cooking Time: 14 minutes   Serves: 4

Ingredients:
- Beets – 4
- Balsamic vinegar – 2 tbsps.
- Parsley – 1 bunch, chopped
- Salt and black pepper to taste
- Extra-virgin olive oil – 1 tbsp.
- Garlic – 1 clove, chopped
- Capers – 2 tbsps.

Directions:
1. Put beets in the air fryer and cook at 360F for 14 minutes. Meanwhile, in a bowl, mix garlic, parsley, olive oil, salt, pepper, and capers and mix well. Remove the beets, and cool. Peel and slice them. Add vinegar, drizzle the parsley dressing over and serve.

Broccoli Salad

Cooking Time: 8 minutes
Serves: 4

Ingredients:
- Broccoli – 1 head, florets separated
- Peanut oil – 1 tbsp.
- Garlic – 6 cloves, minced
- Chinese rice wine vinegar – 1 tbsp.
- Salt and black pepper to taste

Directions:
1. In a bowl, mix broccoli with half of the oil, salt, and pepper and toss. Cook in the air fryer at 350F for 8 minutes. Shake once. Transfer broccoli to a bowl. Add the rest of the peanut oil, rice vinegar, and garlic, and toss well. Serve.

Brussels Sprouts and Tomatoes Mix

Cooking Time: 10 minutes
Serves: 4

Ingredients:
- Brussels sprouts – 1 pound, trimmed
- Salt and black pepper to taste
- Cherry tomatoes – 8, halved
- Green onions – ¼ cup, chopped
- Olive oil – 1 tbsp.

Directions:
1. Season Brussels sprouts with salt and pepper. Cook in the air fryer at 350F for 10 minutes. Transfer to a bowl. Add olive oil, green onions, cherry tomatoes, salt, and pepper. Toss and serve.

Spicy Cabbage

Cooking Time: 8 minutes
Serves: 4

Ingredients:
- Cabbage – 1, cut into 8 wedges
- Sesame seed oil – 1 tbsp.
- Carrot – 1, grated
- Apple cider vinegar – ¼ cup
- Apple juice – ¼ cup
- Cayenne pepper – ½ tsp.
- Red pepper flakes – 1 tsp. crushed

Directions:
1. In a pan, combine cabbage with pepper flakes, cayenne, apple juice, vinegar, carrot, and oil. Toss to mix. Place the pan in the preheated air fryer and cook at 350F for 8 minutes. Divide cabbage mix between plates and serve.

Collard Greens Mix

Cooking Time: 10 minutes	Serves: 4

Ingredients:
- Collard greens – 1 bunch, trimmed
- Olive oil – 2 tbsps.
- Tomato paste – 2 tbsps.
- Yellow onion – 1, chopped
- Garlic – 3 cloves, minced
- Salt and black pepper to taste
- Balsamic vinegar – 1 tbsp.
- Sugar – 1 tsp.

Directions:
1. In a bowl, mix tomato puree, onion, vinegar, garlic, and oil. Whisk. Add sugar, salt, pepper, and collard greens. Mix. Place the bowl in the air fryer and cook at 320F for 10 minutes. Serve.

Eggplant and Zucchini Mix

Cooking Time: 8 minutes	Serves: 4

Ingredients:
- Eggplant – 1, cubed
- Zucchinis – 3, roughly cubed
- Lemon juice - 2 tbsps.
- Salt and black pepper to taste
- Thyme – 1 tsp. dried
- Oregano – 1 tsp. dried
- Olive oil – 3 tbsps.

Directions:
1. Put eggplant in a dish. Add olive oil, oregano, thyme, salt, pepper, lemon juice, and zucchinis. Toss to mix. Place the dish in the air fryer and at 360F for 8 minutes. Serve.

FISH AND SEAFOOD

Tha Fish Cakes With Mango Relish

Cooking Time: 10 minutes
Serves: 4

Ingredients:
- 1 lb White Fish Fillets
- 3 Tbsps Ground Coconut
- 1 Ripened Mango
- ½ Tsps Chili Paste
- Tbsps Fresh Parsley
- 1 Green Onion
- 1 Lime
- 1 Tsp Salt
- 1 Egg

Directions:
1. 1 Preparing the Ingredients. To make the relish, peel and dice the mango into cubes. Combine with a half teaspoon of chili paste, a tablespoon of parsley, and the zest and juice of half a lime.
2. In a food processor, pulse the fish until it forms a smooth texture. Place into a bowl and add the salt, egg, chopped green onion, parsley, two tablespoons of the coconut, and the remainder of the chili paste and lime zest and juice. Combine well
3. Portion the mixture into 10 equal balls and flatten them into small patties. Pour the reserved tablespoon of coconut onto a dish and roll the patties over to coat.
4. Preheat the Instant Crisp Air Fryer to 390 degrees
5. 2 Air Frying. Place the fish cakes into the Instant Crisp Air Fryer, close air fryer lid and cook for 8 minutes. They should be crisp and lightly browned when ready
6. Serve hot with mango relish

Air Fryer Fish Tacos

Cooking Time: 15 minutes
Serves: 4

Ingredients:
- 1 pound cod
- 1 tbsp. cumin
- ½ tbsp. chili powder
- 1 ½ C. almond flour
- 1 ½ C. coconut flour
- 10 ounces Mexican beer
- 2 eggs

Directions:
1. Preparing the Ingredients. Whisk beer and eggs together.
2. Whisk flours, pepper, salt, cumin, and chili powder together.
3. Slice cod into large pieces and coat in egg mixture then flour mixture.
4. Air Frying. Spray bottom of your Instant Crisp Air Fryer basket with olive oil and add coated codpieces, close air fryer lid and cook 15 minutes at 375 degrees.
5. Serve on lettuce leaves topped with homemade salsa.

Firecracker Shrimp

Cooking Time: 8 minutes
Serves: 4

Ingredients:

For the shrimp
- 1 pound raw shrimp, peeled and deveined
- Salt
- Pepper
- 1 egg
- ½ cup all-purpose flour
- ¾ cup panko bread crumbs
- Cooking oil

For the firecracker sauce
- ⅓ cup sour cream
- 2 tablespoons Sriracha
- ¼ cup sweet chili sauce

Directions:

1. 1 Preparing the Ingredients. Season the shrimp with salt and pepper to taste. In a small bowl, beat the egg. In another small bowl, place the flour. In a third small bowl, add the panko bread crumbs.
2. Spray the Instant Crisp Air Fryer basket with cooking oil. Dip the shrimp in the flour, then the egg, and then the bread crumbs. Place the shrimp in the Instant Crisp Air Fryer basket. It is okay to stack them. Spray the shrimp with cooking oil.
3. 2 Air Frying. Close air fryer lid and cook for 4 minutes. Open the Instant Crisp Air Fryer and flip the shrimp. I recommend flipping individually instead of shaking to keep the breading intact. Cook for an additional 4 minutes or until crisp.
4. While the shrimp is cooking, make the firecracker sauce: In a small bowl, combine the sour cream, Sriracha, and sweet chili sauce. Mix well. Serve with the shrimp.

Firecracker Shrimp

Cooking Time: 8 minutes
Serves: 4

Ingredients:

For the shrimp
- 1 pound raw shrimp, peeled and deveined
- Salt
- Pepper
- 1 egg
- ½ cup all-purpose flour
- ¾ cup panko bread crumbs
- Cooking oil

For the firecracker sauce
- ⅓ cup sour cream
- 2 tablespoons Sriracha
- ¼ cup sweet chili sauce

Directions:

1. 1 Preparing the Ingredients. Season the shrimp with salt and pepper to taste. In a small bowl, beat the egg. In another small bowl, place the flour. In a third small bowl, add the panko bread crumbs.
2. Spray the Instant Crisp Air Fryer basket with cooking oil. Dip the shrimp in the flour, then the egg, and then the bread crumbs. Place the shrimp in the Instant Crisp Air Fryer basket. It is okay to stack them. Spray the shrimp with cooking oil.
3. 2 Air Frying. Close air fryer lid and cook for 4 minutes. Open the Instant Crisp Air Fryer and flip the shrimp. I recommend flipping individually instead of shaking to keep the breading intact. Cook for an additional 4 minutes or until crisp.
4. While the shrimp is cooking, make the firecracker sauce: In a small bowl, combine the sour cream, Sriracha, and sweet chili sauce. Mix well. Serve with the shrimp.

Air Fryer Fish Tacos

Cooking Time: 15 minutes
Serves: 4

Ingredients:
- 1 pound cod
- 1 tbsp. cumin
- ½ tbsp. chili powder
- 1 ½ C. almond flour
- 1 ½ C. coconut flour
- 10 ounces Mexican beer
- 2 eggs

Directions:
1. Preparing the Ingredients. Whisk beer and eggs together.
2. Whisk flours, pepper, salt, cumin, and chili powder together.
3. Slice cod into large pieces and coat in egg mixture then flour mixture.
4. Air Frying. Spray bottom of your Instant Crisp Air Fryer basket with olive oil and add coated codpieces, close air fryer lid and cook 15 minutes at 375 degrees.
5. Serve on lettuce leaves topped with homemade salsa.

Sesame Seeds Coated Fish

Cooking Time: 8 minutes
Serves: 5

Ingredients:
- 3 tablespoons plain flour
- 2 eggs
- ½ cup sesame seeds, toasted
- ½ cup breadcrumbs
- 1/8 teaspoon dried rosemary, crushed
- Pinch of salt
- Pinch of black pepper
- 3 tablespoons olive oil
- 5 frozen fish fillets (white fish of your choice)

Directions:
1. 1 Preparing the Ingredients. In a shallow dish, place flour. In a second shallow dish, beat the eggs. In a third shallow dish, add remaining ingredients except fish fillets and mix till a crumbly mixture forms.
2. Coat the fillets with flour and shake off the excess flour.
3. Next, dip the fillets in egg.
4. Then coat the fillets with sesame seeds mixture generously.
5. Preheat the Instant Crisp Air Fryer to 390 degrees F.
6. 2 Air Frying. Line an Instant Crisp Air Fryer basket with a piece of foil. Arrange the fillets into prepared basket. Close air fryer lid and cook for about 14 minutes, flipping once after 10 minutes.

Bacon Wrapped Scallops

Cooking Time: 5 minutes
Serves: 4

Ingredients:
- 1 tsp. paprika
- 1 tsp. lemon pepper
- 5 slices of center-cut bacon
- 20 raw sea scallops

Directions:
1. Preparing the Ingredients. Rinse and drain scallops, placing on paper towels to soak up excess moisture.
2. Cut slices of bacon into 4 pieces.
3. Wrap each scallop with a piece of bacon, using toothpicks to secure. Sprinkle wrapped scallops with paprika and lemon pepper.
4. Air Frying. Spray Instant Crisp Air Fryer basket with olive oil and add scallops. Close air fryer lid and cook 5-6 minutes at 400 degrees, making sure to flip halfway through.

Bacon Wrapped Scallops

Cooking Time: 5 minutes
Serves: 4

Ingredients:
- 1 tsp. paprika
- 1 tsp. lemon pepper
- 5 slices of center-cut bacon
- 20 raw sea scallops

Directions:
1. Preparing the Ingredients. Rinse and drain scallops, placing on paper towels to soak up excess moisture.
2. Cut slices of bacon into 4 pieces.
3. Wrap each scallop with a piece of bacon, using toothpicks to secure. Sprinkle wrapped scallops with paprika and lemon pepper.
4. Air Frying. Spray Instant Crisp Air Fryer basket with olive oil and add scallops. Close air fryer lid and cook 5-6 minutes at 400 degrees, making sure to flip halfway through.

Sesame Seeds Coated Fish

Cooking Time: 8 minutes
Serves: 5

Ingredients:
- 3 tablespoons plain flour
- 2 eggs
- ½ cup sesame seeds, toasted
- ½ cup breadcrumbs
- 1/8 teaspoon dried rosemary, crushed
- Pinch of salt
- Pinch of black pepper
- 3 tablespoons olive oil
- 5 frozen fish fillets (white fish of your choice)

Directions:
1. 1 Preparing the Ingredients. In a shallow dish, place flour. In a second shallow dish, beat the eggs. In a third shallow dish, add remaining ingredients except fish fillets and mix till a crumbly mixture forms.
2. Coat the fillets with flour and shake off the excess flour.
3. Next, dip the fillets in egg.
4. Then coat the fillets with sesame seeds mixture generously.
5. Preheat the Instant Crisp Air Fryer to 390 degrees F.
6. 2 Air Frying. Line an Instant Crisp Air Fryer basket with a piece of foil. Arrange the fillets into prepared basket. Close air fryer lid and cook for about 14 minutes, flipping once after 10 minutes.

Crispy Paprika Fish Fillets

Cooking Time: 15 minutes
Serves: 4

Ingredients:
- 1/2 cup seasoned breadcrumbs
- 1 tablespoon balsamic vinegar
- 1/2 teaspoon seasoned salt
- 1 teaspoon paprika
- 1/2 teaspoon ground black pepper
- 1 teaspoon celery seed
- 2 fish fillets, halved
- 1 egg, beaten

Directions:
1. 1 Preparing the Ingredients. Add the breadcrumbs, vinegar, salt, paprika, ground black pepper, and celery seeds to your food processor. Process for about 30 seconds.
2. Coat the fish fillets with the beaten egg; then, coat them with the breadcrumbs mixture.
3. 2 Air Frying. Close air fryer lid. Cook at 350 degrees F for about 15 minutes.

Parmesan Shrimp

Cooking Time: 10 minutes
Serves: 4

Ingredients:
- 2 tbsp. olive oil
- 1 tsp. onion powder
- 1 tsp. basil
- ½ tsp. oregano
- 1 tsp. pepper
- 2/3 C. grated parmesan cheese
- 4 minced garlic cloves
- pounds of jumbo cooked shrimp (peeled/deveined)

Directions:
1. 1 Preparing the Ingredients. Mix all seasonings together and gently toss shrimp with mixture.
2. 2 Air Frying. Spray olive oil into the Instant Crisp Air Fryer basket and add seasoned shrimp. Close air fryer lid and cook 8-10 minutes at 350 degrees.
3. Squeeze lemon juice over shrimp right before devouring!

Parmesan Shrimp

Cooking Time: 10 minutes
Serves: 4

Ingredients:
- 2 tbsp. olive oil
- 1 tsp. onion powder
- 1 tsp. basil
- ½ tsp. oregano
- 1 tsp. pepper
- 2/3 C. grated parmesan cheese
- 4 minced garlic cloves
- pounds of jumbo cooked shrimp (peeled/deveined)

Directions:
1. 1 Preparing the Ingredients. Mix all seasonings together and gently toss shrimp with mixture.
2. 2 Air Frying. Spray olive oil into the Instant Crisp Air Fryer basket and add seasoned shrimp. Close air fryer lid and cook 8-10 minutes at 350 degrees.
3. Squeeze lemon juice over shrimp right before devouring!

Crispy Paprika Fish Fillets

Cooking Time: 15 minutes
Serves: 4

Ingredients:
- 1/2 cup seasoned breadcrumbs
- 1 tablespoon balsamic vinegar
- 1/2 teaspoon seasoned salt
- 1 teaspoon paprika
- 1/2 teaspoon ground black pepper
- 1 teaspoon celery seed
- 2 fish fillets, halved
- 1 egg, beaten

Directions:
1. 1 Preparing the Ingredients. Add the breadcrumbs, vinegar, salt, paprika, ground black pepper, and celery seeds to your food processor. Process for about 30 seconds.
2. Coat the fish fillets with the beaten egg; then, coat them with the breadcrumbs mixture.
3. 2 Air Frying. Close air fryer lid. Cook at 350 degrees F for about 15 minutes.

Flaky Fish Quesadilla

Cooking Time: 12 minutes   Serves: 4

Ingredients:
- Two 6-inch corn or flour tortilla shells
- 1 medium-sized tilapia fillet, approximately 4 ounces
- ½ medium-sized lemon, sliced
- ½ an avocado, peeled, pitted and sliced
- 1 clove of garlic, peeled and finely minced
- Pinch of salt and pepper
- ½ teaspoon of lemon juice
- ¼ cup of shredded cheddar cheese
- ¼ cup of shredded mozzarella cheese

Directions:
1. 1 Preparing the Ingredients. Preheat the Instant Crisp Air Fryer to 350 degrees.
2. In the oven, grill the tilapia with a little salt and lemon slices in foil on high heat for 20 minutes.
3. Remove fish in foil from the oven, and break the fish meat apart into bite-sized pieces with a fork – it should be flaky and chunky when cooked.
4. While the fish is cooling, combine the avocado, garlic, salt, pepper, and lemon juice in a small mixing bowl; mash lightly, but don't whip - keep the avocado slightly chunky.
5. Spread the guacamole on one of the tortillas, then cover with the fish flakes, and then with the cheese. Top with the second tortilla.
6. Place directly on hot surface of the air frying basket.
7. 2 Air Frying. Close air fryer lid. Set the Instant Crisp Air Fryer timer for 6 minutes. After 6 minutes, when the Instant Crisp Air Fryer shuts off, flip the tortillas onto the other side with a spatula; the cheese should be melted enough that it won't fall apart.
8. Reset Instant Crisp Air Fryer to 350 degrees for another 6 minutes.
9. After 6 minutes, when the Instant Crisp Air Fryer shuts off, the tortillas should be browned and crisp, and the fish, guacamole and cheese will be hot and delicious inside. Remove with spatula and let sit on a serving plate to cool for a few minutes before slicing.

Quick Fried Catfish

Cooking Time: 15 minutes
Serves: 4

Ingredients:
- 3/4 cups Original Bisquick™ mix
- 1/2 cup yellow cornmeal
- 1 tablespoon seafood seasoning
- 4 catfish fillets (4 to 6 ounces each)
- 1/2 cup ranch dressing
- Lemon wedges

Directions:
1. 1 Preparing the Ingredients. In a shallow bowl mix together the Bisquick mix, cornmeal, and seafood seasoning. Pat the filets dry, then brush them with ranch dressing.
2. Press the filets into the Bisquick mix on both sides until the filet is evenly coated.
3. 2 Air Frying. Close air fryer lid and cook in your Instant Crisp Air Fryer at 360 degrees for 15 minutes, flip the filets halfway through.
4. Serve with a lemon garnish.

Honey Glazed Salmon

Cooking Time: 8 minutes
Serves: 2

Ingredients:
- 1 tsp. water
- 3 tsp. rice wine vinegar
- 6 tbsp. low-sodium soy sauce
- 6 tbsp. raw honey
- 2 salmon fillets

Directions:
1. 1 Preparing the Ingredients. Combine water, vinegar, honey, and soy sauce together. Pour half of this mixture into a bowl.
2. Place salmon in one bowl of marinade and let chill 2 hours.
3. 2 Air Frying. Ensure your Instant Crisp Air Fryer is preheated to 356 degrees and add salmon. Close air fryer lid and cook 8 minutes, flipping halfway through. Baste salmon with some of the remaining marinade mixture and cook another 5 minutes.
4. To make a sauce to serve salmon with, pour remaining marinade mixture into a saucepan, heating till simmering. Let simmer 2 minutes. Serve drizzled over salmon!

Fish and Chips

Cooking Time: 20 minutes
Serves: 4

Ingredients:
- 4 (4-ounce) fish fillets
- Pinch salt
- Freshly ground black pepper
- ½ teaspoon dried thyme
- 1 egg white
- ¾ cup crushed potato chips
- 2 tablespoons olive oil, divided
- 3 russet potatoes, peeled and cut into strips

Directions:
1. 1 Preparing the Ingredients. Pat the fish fillets dry and sprinkle with salt, pepper, and thyme. Set aside.
2. In a shallow bowl, beat the egg white until foamy. In another bowl, combine the potato chips and 1 tablespoon of olive oil and mix until combined.
3. Dip the fish fillets into the egg white, then into the crushed potato chip mixture to coat.
4. Toss the fresh potato strips with the remaining 1 tablespoon olive oil.
5. 2 Air Frying. Use your separator to divide the Instant Crisp Air Fryer basket in half, close air fryer lid and fry the chips and fish. The chips will take about 20 minutes; the fish will take about 10 to 12 minutes to cook.

Fish and Chips

Cooking Time: 20 minutes
Serves: 4

Ingredients:
- 4 (4-ounce) fish fillets
- Pinch salt
- Freshly ground black pepper
- ½ teaspoon dried thyme
- 1 egg white
- ¾ cup crushed potato chips
- 2 tablespoons olive oil, divided
- 3 russet potatoes, peeled and cut into strips

Directions:
1. 1 Preparing the Ingredients. Pat the fish fillets dry and sprinkle with salt, pepper, and thyme. Set aside.
2. In a shallow bowl, beat the egg white until foamy. In another bowl, combine the potato chips and 1 tablespoon of olive oil and mix until combined.
3. Dip the fish fillets into the egg white, then into the crushed potato chip mixture to coat.
4. Toss the fresh potato strips with the remaining 1 tablespoon olive oil.
5. 2 Air Frying. Use your separator to divide the Instant Crisp Air Fryer basket in half, close air fryer lid and fry the chips and fish. The chips will take about 20 minutes; the fish will take about 10 to 12 minutes to cook.

Honey Glazed Salmon

Cooking Time: 8 minutes
Serves: 2

Ingredients:
- 1 tsp. water
- 3 tsp. rice wine vinegar
- 6 tbsp. low-sodium soy sauce
- 6 tbsp. raw honey
- 2 salmon fillets

Directions:
1. 1 Preparing the Ingredients. Combine water, vinegar, honey, and soy sauce together. Pour half of this mixture into a bowl.
2. Place salmon in one bowl of marinade and let chill 2 hours.
3. 2 Air Frying. Ensure your Instant Crisp Air Fryer is preheated to 356 degrees and add salmon. Close air fryer lid and cook 8 minutes, flipping halfway through. Baste salmon with some of the remaining marinade mixture and cook another 5 minutes.
4. To make a sauce to serve salmon with, pour remaining marinade mixture into a saucepan, heating till simmering. Let simmer 2 minutes. Serve drizzled over salmon!

Fish Sandwiches

Cooking Time: 20 minutes
Serves: 4

Ingredients:
- lbs White Fish Fillets
- 1/4 Cup Yellow Cornmeal
- 1 Tsp Greek Seasoning
- Salt and Pepper to taste
- 2 ½ Cups Plain Flour
- 2 Tsps Baking Powder
- 2 Cups Beer
- 4 Hamburger Buns
- Mayonnaise
- Lettuce Leaves
- 1 Tomato, sliced
- 1 Egg

Directions:
1. 1 Preparing the Ingredients. Cut the fish fillets into burger patty sized strips. Season with salt and pepper to desired taste.
2. In a medium bowl, mix together the beer, egg, baking powder, plain flour, cornmeal, Greek seasoning and additional salt and pepper
3. Heat the Instant Crisp Air Fryer to 340 degrees
4. Place each seasoned fish strip into the batter, ensuring that it is well coated
5. 2 Air Frying. Place battered fish into the Instant Crisp Air Fryer tray, close air fryer lid and cook in batches for 6 minutes or until crispy
6. Compile the sandwich by topping each bun with mayonnaise, then a lettuce leaf, tomato slices, and finally the cooked fish strip

Crab Cakes

Cooking Time: 10 minutes
Serves: 4

Ingredients:
- 8 ounces jumbo lump crabmeat
- 1 tablespoon Old Bay Seasoning
- ⅓ cup bread crumbs
- ¼ cup diced red bell pepper
- ¼ cup diced green bell pepper
- 1 egg
- ¼ cup mayonnaise
- Juice of ½ lemon
- 1 teaspoon flour
- Cooking oil

Directions:
1. 1 Preparing the Ingredients. In a large bowl, combine the crabmeat, Old Bay Seasoning, bread crumbs, red bell pepper, green bell pepper, egg, mayo, and lemon juice. Mix gently to combine.
2. Form the mixture into 4 patties. Sprinkle ¼ teaspoon of flour on top of each patty.
3. 2 Air Frying. Place the crab cakes in the Instant Crisp Air Fryer. Spray them with cooking oil. Close air fryer lid and cook for 10 minutes.
4. Serve.

Crispy Air Fried Sushi Roll

Cooking Time: 5 minutes
Serves: 12

Ingredients:
- Kale Salad:
- 1 tbsp. sesame seeds
- ¾ tsp. soy sauce
- ¼ tsp. ginger
- 1/8 tsp. garlic powder
- ¾ tsp. toasted sesame oil
- ½ tsp. rice vinegar
- 1 ½ C. chopped kale
- Sushi Rolls:
- ½ of a sliced avocado
- 3 sheets of sushi nori
- 1 batch cauliflower rice
- *Sriracha Mayo:*
- Sriracha sauce
- ¼ C. vegan mayo
- Coating:
- ½ C. panko breadcrumbs

Directions:
1. 1 Preparing the Ingredients. Combine all of kale salad ingredients together, tossing well. Set to the side.
2. Lay out a sheet of nori and spread a handful of rice on. Then place 2-3 tbsp. of kale salad over rice, followed by avocado. Roll up sushi.
3. To make mayo, whisk mayo ingredients together until smooth.
4. Add breadcrumbs to a bowl.
5. 2 Air Frying. Coat sushi rolls in crumbs till coated and add to the Instant Crisp Air Fryer. Close air fryer lid and cook rolls 10 minutes at 390 degrees, shaking gently at 5 minutes.
6. Slice each roll into 6-8 pieces and enjoy!

Alaskan Cod with Pinto Beans & Fennel

Cooking Time: 21 minutes
Serves: 4

Ingredients:
- 2 (18 oz) Alaskan Cod, cut into 4 pieces each
- 4 tbsp Olive Oil
- 2 cloves Garlic, minced
- 2 small Onions, chopped
- ½ cup Olive Brine
- 3 cups Chicken Broth
- Salt and Black Pepper to taste
- ½ cup Tomato Puree
- 1 head Fennel, quartered
- 1 cup Pinto Beans, soaked, drained and rinsed
- 1 cup Green Olives, pitted and crushed
- ½ cup Basil Leaves
- Lemon Slices to garnish

Directions:
1. Select Sear/Sauté and heat olive oil. Stir-fry garlic and onion for 3 minutes. Pour in chicken broth, tomato puree, fennel, olives, beans, salt, and pepper. Seal the lid and select Steam on High pressure for 10 minutes. Press Start.
2. Once the timer has stopped, do a quick pressure release, and open the lid.
3. Transfer the beans to a plate with a slotted spoon. Adjust broth's taste with salt and pepper and add the cod pieces to the cooker.
4. Close the lid again, secure the pressure valve, and select Steam mode on Low pressure for 3 minutes. Press Start.
5. Once the timer has ended, do a quick pressure release, and open the lid.
6. Remove the cod into soup plates, top with the beans and basil leaves, and spoon the broth over them. Serve with a side of crusted bread.

Alaskan Cod with Pinto Beans & Fennel

Cooking Time: 21 minutes
Serves: 4

Ingredients:
- 2 (18 oz) Alaskan Cod, cut into 4 pieces each
- 4 tbsp Olive Oil
- 2 cloves Garlic, minced
- 2 small Onions, chopped
- ½ cup Olive Brine
- 3 cups Chicken Broth
- Salt and Black Pepper to taste
- ½ cup Tomato Puree
- 1 head Fennel, quartered
- 1 cup Pinto Beans, soaked, drained and rinsed
- 1 cup Green Olives, pitted and crushed
- ½ cup Basil Leaves
- Lemon Slices to garnish

Directions:
1. Select Sear/Sauté and heat olive oil. Stir-fry garlic and onion for 3 minutes. Pour in chicken broth, tomato puree, fennel, olives, beans, salt, and pepper. Seal the lid and select Steam on High pressure for 10 minutes. Press Start.
2. Once the timer has stopped, do a quick pressure release, and open the lid.
3. Transfer the beans to a plate with a slotted spoon. Adjust broth's taste with salt and pepper and add the cod pieces to the cooker.
4. Close the lid again, secure the pressure valve, and select Steam mode on Low pressure for 3 minutes. Press Start.
5. Once the timer has ended, do a quick pressure release, and open the lid.
6. Remove the cod into soup plates, top with the beans and basil leaves, and spoon the broth over them. Serve with a side of crusted bread.

Crispy Air Fried Sushi Roll

Cooking Time: 5 minutes
Serves: 12

Ingredients:
- Kale Salad:
- 1 tbsp. sesame seeds
- ¾ tsp. soy sauce
- ¼ tsp. ginger
- 1/8 tsp. garlic powder
- ¾ tsp. toasted sesame oil
- ½ tsp. rice vinegar
- 1 ½ C. chopped kale
- Sushi Rolls:
- ½ of a sliced avocado
- 3 sheets of sushi nori
- 1 batch cauliflower rice
- *Sriracha Mayo:*
- Sriracha sauce
- ¼ C. vegan mayo
- Coating:
- ½ C. panko breadcrumbs

Directions:
1. 1 Preparing the Ingredients. Combine all of kale salad ingredients together, tossing well. Set to the side.
2. Lay out a sheet of nori and spread a handful of rice on. Then place 2-3 tbsp. of kale salad over rice, followed by avocado. Roll up sushi.
3. To make mayo, whisk mayo ingredients together until smooth.
4. Add breadcrumbs to a bowl.
5. 2 Air Frying. Coat sushi rolls in crumbs till coated and add to the Instant Crisp Air Fryer. Close air fryer lid and cook rolls 10 minutes at 390 degrees, shaking gently at 5 minutes.
6. Slice each roll into 6-8 pieces and enjoy!

Scottish Seafood Curry

Cooking Time: 33 minutes   Serves: 8

Ingredients:

Seafood:
- ½ lb Squid, trimmed and cut into 1-inch rings
- ½ lb Langoustine Tall Meat
- ½ lb Mussel Meat
- ½ lb Scallop Meat

Curry:
- 4 tbsp Olive Oil
- 2 cups Shellfish Stock
- 2 Curry Leaves
- 2 tbsp Shallot Puree
- 3 tbsp Yellow Curry Paste
- 2 tbsp Ginger Paste
- 2 tbsp Garlic Paste
- 1 ½ tbsp Chili Powder
- 1 ½ tbsp Chili Paste
- 2 tbsp Lemongrass Paste
- ½ tsp Turmeric Powder
- 2 tsp Shrimp Powder
- 1 tsp Shrimp Paste
- 1 ½ cups Coconut Milk
- 1 cup Milk
- 1 tbsp Grants Scotch Whiskey
- 2 tbsp Fish Curry Powder
- Salt to taste

Vegetables:
- ¼ cup diced Tomatoes
- ¼ cup chopped Onion
- ¼ cup chopped Okra
- ¼ cup chopped Eggplants

Directions:
1. Add olive oil, shallot paste, yellow curry paste, ginger puree, garlic paste, lemongrass paste, chili paste, shrimp paste, and curry leaves.
2. Stir-fry for 10 minutes on Sear/Sauté mode, until well combined and aromatic.
3. Next, add turmeric powder, fish curry powder, and shrimp powder. Stir-fry for another minute. Pour in the shellfish stock and close the crisping lid. Cook on Broil mode for 15 minutes.
4. Open the lid, and add the scallops, squid, chopped onion, okra, tomatoes, and aubergine. Stir lightly. Close the pressure lid, secure the pressure valve, and select Steam mode on High pressure for 5 minutes. Press Start to start

cooking.
5. Once the timer has ended, do a quick pressure release, and open the lid.
6. Add milk, coconut milk, scotch whiskey, and salt. Stir carefully not to mash the aubergine. Select Sear/Sauté and add mussel meat and langoustine. Stir carefully.
7. Simmer the sauce for 3 minutes, press Stop, and turn off the cooker. Dish the seafood with sauce and veggies into serving bowls. Serve with broccoli mash.

Meaditerranean Scallops with Butter-Caper Sauce

Cooking Time: 12 minutes
Serves: 6

Ingredients:
- 2 lb Sea Scallops, foot removed
- 10 tbsp Butter, unsalted
- 4 tbsp Capers, drained
- 4 tbsp Olive Oil
- 1 cup Dry White Wine
- 3 tsp lemon Zest

Directions:
1. Melt the butter to caramel brown on Sear/Sauté. Use a soup spook to fetch the butter out into a bowl.
2. Next, heat the oil in the pot, once heated add the scallops and sear them on both sides to golden brown which is about 5 minutes. Remove to a plate and set aside.
3. Pour the white wine in the pot to deglaze the bottom while using a spoon to scrape the bottom of the pot of any scallop bits.
4. Add the capers, butter, and lemon zest. Use a spoon to stir the mixture once gently. After 40 seconds, spoon the sauce with capers over the scallops. Serve.

White Wine Black Mussels

Cooking Time: 30 minutes
Serves: 4

Ingredients:
- 1 ½ lb Black Mussels, cleaned and de-bearded
- 3 tbsp Olive Oil
- 3 large Chilies, seeded and chopped
- 3 cloves Garlic, peeled and crushed
- 1 White Onion, chopped finely
- 10 Tomatoes, skin removed and chopped
- 4 tbsp Tomato Paste
- 1 cup Dry White Wine
- 3 cups Vegetable Broth
- ⅓ cup fresh Basil Leaves
- 1 cup fresh Parsley Leaves

Directions:
1. Heat the olive oil on Sear/Sauté mode, and stir-fry the onion, until soft. Add the chilies and garlic, and cook for 2 minutes, stirring frequently.
2. Stir in the tomatoes and tomato paste, and cook for 2 more minutes. Then, pour in the wine and vegetable broth. Let simmer for 5 minutes.
3. Add the mussels, close the lid, secure the pressure valve, and press Steam mode on High pressure for 3 minutes. Press Start to start cooking.
4. Once the timer has ended, do a natural pressure release for 15 minutes, then a quick pressure release, and open the lid.
5. Remove and discard any unopened mussels. Then, add half of the basil and parsley, and stir. Close the crisping lid and cook on Broil mode for 5 minutes.
6. Dish the mussels with sauce in serving bowls and garnish it with the remaining basil and parsley. Serve with a side of crusted bread.

POULTRY RECIPES

Tex-Mex Turkey Burgers

Cooking Time: 15 minutes
Serves: 4

Ingredients:
- ⅓ cup finely crushed corn tortilla chips
- 1 egg, beaten
- ¼ cup salsa
- ⅓ cup shredded pepper Jack cheese
- Pinch salt
- Freshly ground black pepper
- 1 pound ground turkey
- 1 tablespoon olive oil
- 1 teaspoon paprika

Directions:
1. Preparing the Ingredients. In a medium bowl, combine the tortilla chips, egg, salsa, cheese, salt, and pepper, and mix well.
2. Add the turkey and mix gently but thoroughly with clean hands.
3. Form the meat mixture into patties about ½ inch thick. Make an indentation in the center of each patty with your thumb so the burgers don't puff up while cooking.
4. Brush the patties on both sides with the olive oil and sprinkle with paprika.
5. Air Frying. Put in the Instant Crisp Air Fryer basket, lock the air fryer lid and Grill for 14 to 16 minutes or until the meat registers at least 165°F.

POULTRY RECIPES

Tex-Mex Turkey Burgers

Cooking Time: 15 minutes
Serves: 4

Ingredients:
- ⅓ cup finely crushed corn tortilla chips
- 1 egg, beaten
- ¼ cup salsa
- ⅓ cup shredded pepper Jack cheese
- Pinch salt
- Freshly ground black pepper
- 1 pound ground turkey
- 1 tablespoon olive oil
- 1 teaspoon paprika

Directions:
1. Preparing the Ingredients. In a medium bowl, combine the tortilla chips, egg, salsa, cheese, salt, and pepper, and mix well.
2. Add the turkey and mix gently but thoroughly with clean hands.
3. Form the meat mixture into patties about ½ inch thick. Make an indentation in the center of each patty with your thumb so the burgers don't puff up while cooking.
4. Brush the patties on both sides with the olive oil and sprinkle with paprika.
5. Air Frying. Put in the Instant Crisp Air Fryer basket, lock the air fryer lid and Grill for 14 to 16 minutes or until the meat registers at least 165°F.

White Wine Black Mussels

Cooking Time: 30 minutes
Serves: 4

Ingredients:
- 1 ½ lb Black Mussels, cleaned and de-bearded
- 3 tbsp Olive Oil
- 3 large Chilies, seeded and chopped
- 3 cloves Garlic, peeled and crushed
- 1 White Onion, chopped finely
- 10 Tomatoes, skin removed and chopped
- 4 tbsp Tomato Paste
- 1 cup Dry White Wine
- 3 cups Vegetable Broth
- ⅓ cup fresh Basil Leaves
- 1 cup fresh Parsley Leaves

Directions:
1. Heat the olive oil on Sear/Sauté mode, and stir-fry the onion, until soft. Add the chilies and garlic, and cook for 2 minutes, stirring frequently.
2. Stir in the tomatoes and tomato paste, and cook for 2 more minutes. Then, pour in the wine and vegetable broth. Let simmer for 5 minutes.
3. Add the mussels, close the lid, secure the pressure valve, and press Steam mode on High pressure for 3 minutes. Press Start to start cooking.
4. Once the timer has ended, do a natural pressure release for 15 minutes, then a quick pressure release, and open the lid.
5. Remove and discard any unopened mussels. Then, add half of the basil and parsley, and stir. Close the crisping lid and cook on Broil mode for 5 minutes.
6. Dish the mussels with sauce in serving bowls and garnish it with the remaining basil and parsley. Serve with a side of crusted bread.

Air Fryer Turkey Breast

Cooking Time: 60 minutes
Serves: 6

Ingredients:
- Pepper and salt
- 1 oven-ready turkey breast
- Turkey seasonings of choice

Directions:
1. 1 Preparing the Ingredients. Preheat the Instant Crisp Air Fryer to 350 degrees.
2. Season turkey with pepper, salt, and other desired seasonings.
3. Place turkey in Instant Crisp Air Fryer basket.
4. 2 Air Frying. Lock the air fryer lid. Set temperature to 350°F, and set time to 60 minutes. Cook 60 minutes. The meat should be at 165 degrees when done.
5. Allow to rest 10-15 minutes before slicing. Enjoy!

Cheese Stuffed Chicken

Cooking Time: 30 minutes
Serves: 4

Ingredients:
- 1 tablespoon creole seasoning
- 1 tablespoon olive oil
- 1 teaspoon garlic powder
- 1 teaspoon onion powder
- 4 chicken breasts, butterflied and pounded
- 4 slices Colby cheese
- 4 slices pepper jack cheese

Directions:
1. 1 Preparing the Ingredients. Preheat the Instant Crisp Air Fryer to 390°F.
2. Place the grill pan accessory in the Instant Crisp Air Fryer.
3. Create the dry rub by mixing in a bowl the creole seasoning, garlic powder, and onion powder. Season with salt and pepper if desired.
4. Rub the seasoning on to the chicken.
5. Place the chicken on a working surface and place a slice each of pepper jack and Colby cheese.
6. Fold the chicken and secure the edges with toothpicks.
7. Brush chicken with olive oil.
8. 2 Air Frying. Lock the air fryer lid. Grill for 30 minutes and make sure to flip the meat every 10 minutes.

Orange Curried Chicken Stir-Fry

Cooking Time: 18 minutes
Serves: 4

Ingredients:
- ¾ pound boneless, skinless chicken thighs, cut into 1-inch pieces
- 1 yellow bell pepper, cut into 1½-inch pieces
- 1 small red onion, sliced
- Olive oil for misting
- ¼ cup chicken stock
- 2 tablespoons honey
- ¼ cup orange juice
- 1 tablespoon cornstarch
- 3 to 3 teaspoons curry powder

Directions:
1. Preparing the Ingredients. Put the chicken thighs, pepper, and red onion in the Instant Crisp Air Fryer basket and mist with olive oil.
2. Air Frying. Lock the air fryer lid. Cook for 12 to 14 minutes or until the chicken is cooked to 165°F, shaking the basket halfway through cooking time.
3. Remove the chicken and vegetables from the Instant Crisp Air Fryer basket and set aside.
4. In a 6-inch metal bowl, combine the stock, honey, orange juice, cornstarch, and curry powder, and mix well. Add the chicken and vegetables, stir, and put the bowl in the basket.
5. Return the basket to the Instant Crisp Air Fryer and cook for 2 minutes. Remove and stir, then cook for 2 to 3 minutes or until the sauce is thickened and bubbly.

Mustard Chicken Tenders

Cooking Time: 20 minutes
Serves: 4

Ingredients:
- ½ C. coconut flour
- 1 tbsp. spicy brown mustard
- 2 beaten eggs
- 1 pound of chicken tenders

Directions:
1. 1 Preparing the Ingredients. Season tenders with pepper and salt.
2. Place a thin layer of mustard onto tenders and then dredge in flour and dip in egg.
3. 2 Air Frying. Add to the Instant Crisp Air Fryer, lock the air fryer lid, set temperature to 390°F, and set time to 20 minutes.

Chicken Pot Pie with Coconut Milk

Cooking Time: 30 minutes
Serves: 8

Ingredients:
- ¼ small onion, chopped
- ½ cup broccoli, chopped
- ¾ cup coconut milk
- 1 cup chicken broth
- 1/3 cup coconut flour
- 1-pound ground chicken
- 2 cloves of garlic, minced
- 2 tablespoons butter
- 4 ½ tablespoons butter, melted
- 4 eggs
- Salt and pepper to taste

Directions:
1. 1 Preparing the Ingredients. Preheat the Instant Crisp Air Fryer for 5 minutes.
2. Place 2 tablespoons butter, broccoli, onion, garlic, coconut milk, chicken broth, and ground chicken in a baking dish that will fit in the Instant Crisp Air Fryer. Season with salt and pepper to taste.
3. In a mixing bowl, combine the butter, coconut flour, and eggs.
4. Sprinkle evenly the top of the chicken and broccoli mixture with the coconut flour dough.
5. Place the dish in the Instant Crisp Air Fryer.
6. 2 Air Frying. Lock the air fryer lid. Cook for 30 minutes at 325°F.

Chicken Nuggets

Cooking Time: 20 minutes
Serves: 4

Ingredients:
- 1 pound boneless, skinless chicken breasts
- Chicken seasoning or rub
- Salt
- Pepper
- 2 eggs
- 6 tablespoons bread crumbs
- 2 tablespoons panko bread crumbs
- Cooking oil

Directions:
1. Preparing the Ingredients. Cut the chicken breasts into 1-inch pieces.
2. In a large bowl, combine the chicken pieces with chicken seasoning, salt, and pepper to taste.
3. In a small bowl, beat the eggs. In another bowl, combine the bread crumbs and panko.
4. Dip the chicken pieces in the eggs and then the bread crumbs.
5. Place the nuggets in the Instant Crisp Air Fryer. Do not overcrowd the basket. Cook in batches. Spray the nuggets with cooking oil.
6. Air Frying. Lock the air fryer lid. Cook for 4 minutes. Open the Instant Crisp Air Fryer and shake the basket. Cook for an additional 4 minutes. Remove the cooked nuggets from the Instant Crisp Air Fryer, then repeat for the remaining chicken nuggets. Cool before serving.

Cheesy Chicken Fritters

Cooking Time: 20 minutes
Serves: 17

Ingredients:
- Chicken Fritters:
- ½ tsp. salt
- 1/8 tsp. pepper
- 1 ½ tbsp. fresh dill
- 1 1/3 C. shredded mozzarella cheese
- 1/3 C. coconut flour
- 1/3 C. vegan mayo
- 2 eggs
- 1 ½ pounds chicken breasts
- Garlic Dip:
- 1/8 tsp. pepper
- ¼ tsp. salt
- ½ tbsp. lemon juice
- 1 pressed garlic cloves
- 1/3 C. vegan mayo

Directions:
1. 1 Preparing the Ingredients. Slice chicken breasts into 1/3" pieces and place in a bowl. Add all remaining fritter ingredients to the bowl and stir well. Cover and chill 2 hours or overnight.
2. Ensure your Instant Crisp Air Fryer is preheated to 350 degrees. Spray basket with a bit of olive oil.
3. 2 Air Frying. Add marinated chicken to Instant Crisp Air Fryer. Lock the air fryer lid, set temperature to 350°F, and set time to 20 minutes and cook 20 minutes, making sure to turn halfway through cooking process.
4. To make the dipping sauce, combine all the dip ingredients until smooth.

Chicken BBQ with Sweet And Sour Sauce

Cooking Time: 40 minutes
Serves: 6

Ingredients:
- ¼ cup minced garlic
- ¼ cup tomato paste
- ¾ cup minced onion
- ¾ cup sugar
- 1 cup soy sauce
- 1 cup water
- 1 cup white vinegar
- 6 chicken drumsticks
- Salt and pepper to taste

Directions:
1. 1 Preparing the Ingredients. Place all Ingredients in a Ziploc bag
2. Allow to marinate for at least 2 hours in the fridge.
3. Preheat the Instant Crisp Air Fryer to 390°F.
4. Place the grill pan accessory in the Instant Crisp Air Fryer.
5. 2 Air Frying. Lock the air fryer lid. Grill the chicken for 40 minutes.
6. Flip the chicken every 10 minutes for even grilling.
7. Meanwhile, pour the marinade in a saucepan and heat over medium flame until the sauce thickens.
8. Before serving the chicken, brush with the glaze.

Crusted Chicken Tenders

Cooking Time: 15 minutes
Serves: 3

Ingredients:
- ½ cup all-purpose flour
- 2 eggs, beaten
- ½ cup seasoned breadcrumbs
- Salt and freshly ground black pepper, to taste
- 2 tablespoons olive oil
- ¾ pound chicken tenders

Directions:
1. 1 Preparing the Ingredients. In a bowl, place the flour.
2. In a second bowl, place the eggs.
3. In a third bowl, mix together breadcrumbs, salt, black pepper and oil.
4. Coat the chicken tenders in the flour,
5. Then dip into the eggs and finally coat with the breadcrumbs mixture evenly.
6. 2 Air Frying. Preheat the Instant Crisp Air Fryer to 330 degrees F. Arrange the chicken tenderloins in Instant Crisp Air Fryer basket. Lock the air fryer lid. Cook for about 10 minutes.
7. Now, set the Instant Crisp Air Fryer to 390 degrees F.
8. Cook for about 5 minutes further.

Air Fryer Chicken Parmesan

Cooking Time: 9 minutes
Serves: 4

Ingredients:
- ½ C. keto marinara
- 6 tbsp. mozzarella cheese
- 1 tbsp. melted ghee
- 2 tbsp. grated parmesan cheese
- 6 tbsp. gluten-free seasoned breadcrumbs
- 1 8-ounce chicken breasts

Directions:
1. 1 Preparing the Ingredients. Ensure Instant Crisp Air Fryer is preheated to 360 degrees. Spray the basket with olive oil.
2. Mix parmesan cheese and breadcrumbs together. Melt ghee.
3. Brush melted ghee onto the chicken and dip into breadcrumb mixture.
4. Place coated chicken in the Instant Crisp Air Fryer and top with olive oil.
5. 2 Air Frying. Lock the air fryer lid. Set temperature to 360°F, and set time to 6 minutes. Cook 2 breasts for 6 minutes and top each breast with a tablespoon of sauce and 1½ tablespoons of mozzarella cheese. Cook another 3 minutes to melt cheese.
6. Keep cooked pieces warm as you repeat the process with remaining breasts.

Chicken BBQ Recipe from Peru

Cooking Time: 40 minutes
Serves: 4

Ingredients:
- ½ teaspoon dried oregano
- 1 teaspoon paprika
- 1/3 cup soy sauce
- 2 ½ pounds chicken, quartered
- 2 tablespoons fresh lime juice
- 2 teaspoons ground cumin
- 5 cloves of garlic, minced

Directions:
1. 1 Preparing the Ingredients. Place all Ingredients in a Ziploc bag and shake to mix everything.
2. Allow to marinate for at least 2 hours in the fridge.
3. Preheat the Instant Crisp Air Fryer to 390°F.
4. Place the grill pan accessory in the Instant Crisp Air Fryer.
5. 2 Air Frying. Lock the air fryer lid. Grill the chicken for 40 minutes making sure to flip the chicken every 10 minutes for even grilling.

Ricotta and Parsley Stuffed Turkey Breasts

Cooking Time: 25 minutes
Serves: 4

Ingredients:
- 1 turkey breast, quartered
- 1 cup Ricotta cheese
- 1/4 cup fresh Italian parsley, chopped
- 1 teaspoon garlic powder
- 1/2 teaspoon cumin powder
- 1 egg, beaten
- 1 teaspoon paprika
- Salt and ground black pepper, to taste
- Crushed tortilla chips
- 1 ½ tablespoons extra-virgin olive oil

Directions:
1. 1 Preparing the Ingredients. Firstly, flatten out each piece of turkey breast with a rolling pin. Prepare three mixing bowls.
2. In a shallow bowl, combine Ricotta cheese with the parsley, garlic powder, and cumin powder.
3. Place the Ricotta/parsley mixture in the middle of each piece. Repeat with the remaining pieces of the turkey breast and roll them up.
4. In another shallow bowl, whisk the egg together with paprika. In the third shallow bowl, combine the salt, pepper, and crushed tortilla chips.
5. Dip each roll in the whisked egg, then, roll them over the tortilla chips mixture.
6. Transfer prepared rolls to the Instant Crisp Air Fryer basket. Drizzle olive oil over all.
7. 2 Air Frying. Lock the air fryer lid. Cook at 350 degrees F for 25 minutes, working in batches. Serve warm, garnished with some extra parsley, if desired.

Cheesy Turkey-Rice with Broccoli

Cooking Time: 40 minutes
Serves: 4

Ingredients:
- 1 cup cooked, chopped turkey meat
- 1 tablespoon and 1-1/2 teaspoons butter, melted
- 1/2 (10 ounce) package frozen broccoli, thawed
- 1/2 (7 ounce) package whole wheat crackers, crushed
- 1/2 cup shredded Cheddar cheese
- 1/2 cup uncooked white rice

Directions:
1. 1 Preparing the Ingredients. Bring to a boil 2 cups of water in a saucepan. Stir in rice and simmer for 20 minutes. Turn off fire and set aside.
2. Lightly grease baking pan of Instant Crisp Air Fryer with cooking spray. Mix in cooked rice, cheese, broccoli, and turkey. Toss well to mix.
3. Mix well melted butter and crushed crackers in a small bowl. Evenly spread on top of rice.
4. 2 Air Frying. Lock the air fryer lid. For 20 minutes, cook on 360°F until tops are lightly browned.
5. Serve and enjoy.

Jerk Chicken Wings

Cooking Time: 16 minutes
Serves: 6

Ingredients:
- 1 tsp. salt
- ½ C. red wine vinegar
- 5 tbsp. lime juice
- 4 chopped scallions
- 1 tbsp. grated ginger
- 2 tbsp. brown sugar
- 1 tbsp. chopped thyme
- 1 tsp. white pepper
- 1 tsp. cayenne pepper
- 1 tsp. cinnamon
- 1 tbsp. allspice
- 1 Habanero pepper (seeds/ribs removed and chopped finely)
- 6 chopped garlic cloves
- 2 tbsp. low-sodium soy sauce
- 2 tbsp. olive oil
- 4 pounds of chicken wings

Directions:
1. Preparing the Ingredients. Combine all ingredients except wings in a bowl. Pour into a gallon bag and add chicken wings. Chill 2-24 hours to marinate.
2. Ensure your Instant Crisp Air Fryer is preheated to 390 degrees.
3. Place chicken wings into a strainer to drain excess liquids.
4. Air Frying. Pour half of the wings into your Instant Crisp Air Fryer. Lock the air fryer lid. Set temperature to 390°F, and set time to 16 minutes and cook 14-16 minutes, making sure to shake halfway through the cooking process.
5. Remove and repeat the process with remaining wings.

Jerk Chicken Wings

Cooking Time: 16 minutes
Serves: 6

Ingredients:
- 1 tsp. salt
- ½ C. red wine vinegar
- 5 tbsp. lime juice
- 4 chopped scallions
- 1 tbsp. grated ginger
- 2 tbsp. brown sugar
- 1 tbsp. chopped thyme
- 1 tsp. white pepper
- 1 tsp. cayenne pepper
- 1 tsp. cinnamon
- 1 tbsp. allspice
- 1 Habanero pepper (seeds/ribs removed and chopped finely)
- 6 chopped garlic cloves
- 2 tbsp. low-sodium soy sauce
- 2 tbsp. olive oil
- 4 pounds of chicken wings

Directions:
1. Preparing the Ingredients. Combine all ingredients except wings in a bowl. Pour into a gallon bag and add chicken wings. Chill 2-24 hours to marinate.
2. Ensure your Instant Crisp Air Fryer is preheated to 390 degrees.
3. Place chicken wings into a strainer to drain excess liquids.
4. Air Frying. Pour half of the wings into your Instant Crisp Air Fryer. Lock the air fryer lid. Set temperature to 390°F, and set time to 16 minutes and cook 14-16 minutes, making sure to shake halfway through the cooking process.
5. Remove and repeat the process with remaining wings.

Cheesy Turkey-Rice with Broccoli

Cooking Time: 40 minutes
Serves: 4

Ingredients:
- 1 cup cooked, chopped turkey meat
- 1 tablespoon and 1-1/2 teaspoons butter, melted
- 1/2 (10 ounce) package frozen broccoli, thawed
- 1/2 (7 ounce) package whole wheat crackers, crushed
- 1/2 cup shredded Cheddar cheese
- 1/2 cup uncooked white rice

Directions:
1. 1 Preparing the Ingredients. Bring to a boil 2 cups of water in a saucepan. Stir in rice and simmer for 20 minutes. Turn off fire and set aside.
2. Lightly grease baking pan of Instant Crisp Air Fryer with cooking spray. Mix in cooked rice, cheese, broccoli, and turkey. Toss well to mix.
3. Mix well melted butter and crushed crackers in a small bowl. Evenly spread on top of rice.
4. 2 Air Frying. Lock the air fryer lid. For 20 minutes, cook on 360°F until tops are lightly browned.
5. Serve and enjoy.

BEEF, LAMB AND PORK

Meatloaf

Cooking Time: 25 minutes
Serves: 4

Ingredients:
- Lean beef – 1 pound
- Egg – 1, beaten
- Breadcrumbs – 3 tbsps.
- Onion – 1, chopped
- Fresh thyme – 1 tbsp. chopped
- Salt and pepper to taste
- Mushrooms – 2, sliced
- Olive oil -1 tbsp.

Directions:
1. Combine egg, beef, breadcrumbs, salt, thyme, onion, and pepper in a bowl. Mix well. Place the mixture to a baking pan and mix in the mushrooms. Coat this mix with oil and cook in the air fryer at 380F for 25 minutes. Cool, slice and serve.

Pork Chops

Cooking Time: 20 minutes
Serves: 4

Ingredients:
- Boneless pork chops – 4
- Shredded parmesan cheese – 7 tbsps.
- Salt and pepper to taste
- Paprika – 1 tsp.
- Garlic powder – 1 tsp.
- Onion powder – 1 tsp.
- Oil – 2 tbsps.

Directions:
1. Coat the meat with oil. Combine the Parmesan with all the spices. Rub the meat with this mixture. Cook in the air fryer at 380F for 20 minutes. Flip at the halfway mark. Serve.

Tender Beef with Sour Cream Sauce

Cooking Time: 12 minutes • TOTAL: 17 minutes
Serves: 2

Ingredients:
- 9 ounces tender beef, chopped
- 1 cup scallions, chopped
- 2 cloves garlic, smashed
- 3/4 cup sour cream
- 3/4 teaspoon salt
- 1/4 teaspoon black pepper, or to taste
- 1/2 teaspoon dried dill weed

Directions:
1. 1 Preparing the Ingredients. Add the beef, scallions, and garlic to the baking dish.
2. 2 Air Frying. Close air fryer lid. Cook for about 5 minutes at 390 degrees F.
3. Once the meat is starting to tender, pour in the sour cream. Stir in the salt, black pepper, and dill.
4. Now, cook 7 minutes longer.

Beef Empanadas

Cooking Time: 20 minutes
Serves: 6

Ingredients
- 1 tsp. water
- 1 egg white
- 1 C. picadillo
- 8 Goya empanada discs (thawed)

Directions:
1. 1 Preparing the Ingredients. Ensure your Instant Crisp Air Fryer is preheated to 325. Spray basket with olive oil.
2. Place 2 tablespoons of picadillo into the center of each disc. Fold disc in half and use a fork to seal edges. Repeat with all ingredients.
3. Whisk egg white with water and brush tops of empanadas with egg wash.
4. Add 2-3 empanadas to the Instant Crisp Air Fryer.
5. 2 Air Frying. Close air fryer lid. Set temperature to 325°F, and set time to 8 minutes, cook until golden. Repeat till you cook all filled empanadas.

Beef Pot Pie

Cooking Time: 90 minutes
Serves: 2

Ingredients
- 1 tablespoon olive oil
- 1 pound beef stewing steak, cubed
- 1 large onion, chopped
- 1 tablespoon tomato puree
- 1 can ale
- Warm water, as required
- 2 beef bouillon cubes
- Salt and freshly ground black pepper, to taste
- 1 tablespoon plain flour plus more for dusting
- 1 prepared short crust pastry

Directions:
1. 1 Preparing the Ingredients. In a pan, heat oil on medium heat. Add steak and cook for about 4-5 minutes. Add onion and cook for about 4-5 minutes.
2. Add tomato puree and cook for about 2-3 minutes.
3. In a jug, add the ale and enough water to double the mixture.
4. Add the ale mixture, cubes, salt and black pepper in the pan with beef and bring to a boil on high heat. Reduce the heat to low and simmer for about 1 hour.
5. In a bowl, mix together flour and 3 tablespoons of warm water.
6. Slowly, add the flour mixture in beef mixture, stirring continuously.
7. Remove from heat and keep aside. Roll out the short crust pastry.
8. Line 2 ramekins with pastry and dust with flour.
9. Divide the beef mixture in the ramekins evenly.
10. Place extra pastry on top.
11. 2 Air Frying. Preheat the Instant Crisp Air Fryer to 390 degrees F, close air fryer lid and Cook for about 10 minutes.
12. Now, set the Instant Crisp Air Fryer to 335 degrees F, and Cook for about 6 minutes more.

Bolognaise Sauce

Cooking Time: 30 minutes
Serves: 2

Ingredients
- 13 Ozs Ground Beef
- 1 Carrot
- 1 Stalk of Celery
- 10 Ozs Diced Tomatoes
- 1/2 Onion
- Salt and Pepper to taste
- Oven safe bowl

Directions:
1. 1 Preparing the Ingredients. Preheat the Instant Crisp Air Fryer to 390 degrees.
2. Finely dice the carrot, celery and onions. Place into the oven safe bowl along with the ground beef and combine well
3. 2 Air Frying. Place the bowl into the Instant Crisp Air Fryer tray, close air fryer lid and cook for 12 minutes until browned.
4. Pour the diced tomatoes into the bowl and replace in the Instant Crisp Air Fryer.
5. Season with salt and pepper, then cook for another 18 minutes
6. Serve over cooked pasta or freeze for later use.

Breaded Spam Steaks

Cooking Time: 5 minutes
Serves: 2

Ingredients
- 12 Oz Can Luncheon Meat
- 1 Cup All Purpose Flour
- 2 Eggs, beaten
- 2 Cups Italian Seasoned Breadcrumbs

Directions:
1. 1 Preparing the Ingredients. Preheat the Instant Crisp Air Fryer to 380 degrees.
2. Cut the luncheon meat into 1/4 inch slices.
3. Gently press the luncheon meat slices into the flour to coat and shake off the excess flour. Dip into the beaten egg, then press into breadcrumbs.
4. 2 Air Frying. Place the battered slices into the Instant Crisp Air Fryer tray, close air fryer lid and cook for 3 to 5 minutes until golden brown.
5. Serve with chili or tomato sauce

Air Fryer Burgers

Cooking Time: 10 minutes
Serves: 4

Ingredients:
- 1 pound lean ground beef
- 1 tsp. dried parsley
- ½ tsp. dried oregano
- ½ tsp. pepper
- ½ tsp. salt
- ½ tsp. onion powder
- ½ tsp. garlic powder
- Few drops of liquid smoke
- 1 tsp. Worcestershire sauce

Directions:
1. 1 Preparing the Ingredients. Ensure your Instant Crisp Air Fryer is preheated to 350 degrees.
2. Mix all seasonings together till combined.
3. Place beef in a bowl and add seasonings. Mix well, but do not overmix.
4. Make 4 patties from the mixture and using your thumb, making an indent in the center of each patty.
5. Add patties to Instant Crisp Air Fryer basket.
6. 2 Air Frying. Close air fryer lid. Set temperature to 350°F, and set time to 10 minutes, and cook 10 minutes. No need to turn.

Cheese-Stuffed Meatballs

Cooking Time: 10 minutes
Serves: 4

Ingredients:
- ⅓ cup soft bread crumbs
- 3 tablespoons milk
- 1 tablespoon ketchup
- 1 egg
- ½ teaspoon dried marjoram
- Pinch salt
- Freshly ground black pepper
- 1 pound 95 percent lean ground beef
- 20 ½-inch cubes of cheese
- Olive oil for misting

Directions:
1. 1 Preparing the Ingredients. In a large bowl, combine the bread crumbs, milk, ketchup, egg, marjoram, salt, and pepper, and mix well. Add the ground beef and mix gently but thoroughly with your hands. Form the mixture into 20 meatballs. Shape each meatball around a cheese cube. Mist the meatballs with olive oil and put into the Instant Crisp Air Fryer basket.
2. 2 Air Frying. Close air fryer lid. Bake for 10 to 13 minutes or until the meatballs register 165°F on a meat thermometer.

Roasted Stuffed Peppers

Cooking Time: 20 minutes
Serves: 4

Ingredients:
- 4 ounces shredded cheddar cheese
- ½ tsp. pepper
- ½ tsp. salt
- 1 tsp. Worcestershire sauce
- ½ C. tomato sauce
- 8 ounces lean ground beef
- 1 tsp. olive oil
- 1 minced garlic clove
- ½ chopped onion
- 2 green peppers

Directions:
1. 1 Preparing the Ingredients. Ensure your Instant Crisp Air Fryer is preheated to 390 degrees. Spray with olive oil.
2. Cut stems off bell peppers and remove seeds. Cook in boiling salted water for 3 minutes.
3. Sauté garlic and onion together in a skillet until golden in color.
4. Take skillet off the heat. Mix pepper, salt, Worcestershire sauce, ¼ cup of tomato sauce, half of cheese and beef together.
5. Divide meat mixture into pepper halves. Top filled peppers with remaining cheese and tomato sauce.
6. Place filled peppers in the Instant Crisp Air Fryer.
7. 2 Air Frying. Close air fryer lid. Set temperature to 390°F, and set time to 20 minutes, bake 15-20 minutes.

Air Fried Steak Sandwich

Cooking Time: 16 minutes   Serves: 4

Ingredients:
- Large hoagie bun, sliced in half
- 6 ounces of sirloin or flank steak, sliced into bite-sized pieces
- ½ tablespoon of mustard powder
- ½ tablespoon of soy sauce
- 1 tablespoon of fresh bleu cheese, crumbled
- 8 medium-sized cherry tomatoes, sliced in half
- 1 cup of fresh arugula, rinsed and patted dry

Directions:
1. 1 Preparing the Ingredients. In a small mixing bowl, combine the soy sauce and onion powder; stir with a fork until thoroughly combined.
2. Lay the raw steak strips in the soy-mustard mixture, and fully immerse each piece to marinate.
3. Set the Instant Crisp Air Fryer to 320 degrees for 10 minutes.
4. Arrange the soy-mustard marinated steak pieces on a piece of tin foil, flat and not overlapping, and set the tin foil on one side of the Instant Crisp Air Fryer basket. The foil should not take up more than half of the surface.
5. Lay the hoagie-bun halves, crusty-side up and soft-side down, on the other half of the air-fryer. 2 Air Frying. Close air fryer lid.
6. After 10 minutes, the Instant Crisp Air Fryer will shut off; the hoagie buns should be starting to crisp and the steak will have begun to cook.
7. Carefully, flip the hoagie buns so they are now crusty-side down and soft-side up; crumble a layer of the bleu cheese on each hoagie half.
8. With a long spoon, gently stir the marinated steak in the foil to ensure even coverage. Set the Instant Crisp Air Fryer to 360 degrees for 6 minutes.
9. After 6 minutes, when the fryer shuts off, the bleu cheese will be perfectly melted over the toasted bread, and the steak will be juicy on the inside and crispy on the outside.
10. Remove the cheesy hoagie halves first, using tongs, and set on a serving plate; then cover one side with the steak, and top with the cherry-tomato halves and the arugula. Close with the other cheesy hoagie-half, slice into two pieces, and enjoy.

Carrot and Beef Cocktail Balls

Cooking Time: 20 minutes
Serves: 10

Ingredients:
- 1 pound ground beef
- 2 carrots
- 1 red onion, peeled and chopped
- 2 cloves garlic
- 1/2 teaspoon dried rosemary, crushed
- 1/2 teaspoon dried basil
- 1 teaspoon dried oregano
- 1 egg
- 3/4 cup breadcrumbs
- 1/2 teaspoon salt
- 1/2 teaspoon black pepper, or to taste
- 1 cup plain flour

Directions:
1. 1 Preparing the Ingredients. Place ground beef in a large bowl. In a food processor, pulse the carrot, onion and garlic; transfer the vegetable mixture to a large-sized bowl.
2. Then, add the rosemary, basil, oregano, egg, breadcrumbs, salt, and black pepper.
3. Shape the mixture into even balls; refrigerate for about 30 minutes. Roll the balls into the flour.
4. 2 Air Frying. Close air fryer lid. Then, air-fry the balls at 350 degrees F for about 20 minutes, turning occasionally; work with batches. Serve with toothpicks.

Carrot and Beef Cocktail Balls

Cooking Time: 20 minutes
Serves: 10

Ingredients:
- 1 pound ground beef
- 2 carrots
- 1 red onion, peeled and chopped
- 2 cloves garlic
- 1/2 teaspoon dried rosemary, crushed
- 1/2 teaspoon dried basil
- 1 teaspoon dried oregano
- 1 egg
- 3/4 cup breadcrumbs
- 1/2 teaspoon salt
- 1/2 teaspoon black pepper, or to taste
- 1 cup plain flour

Directions:
1. 1 Preparing the Ingredients. Place ground beef in a large bowl. In a food processor, pulse the carrot, onion and garlic; transfer the vegetable mixture to a large-sized bowl.
2. Then, add the rosemary, basil, oregano, egg, breadcrumbs, salt, and black pepper.
3. Shape the mixture into even balls; refrigerate for about 30 minutes. Roll the balls into the flour.
4. 2 Air Frying. Close air fryer lid. Then, air-fry the balls at 350 degrees F for about 20 minutes, turning occasionally; work with batches. Serve with toothpicks.

Air Fried Steak Sandwich

Cooking Time: 16 minutes   Serves: 4

Ingredients:
- Large hoagie bun, sliced in half
- 6 ounces of sirloin or flank steak, sliced into bite-sized pieces
- ½ tablespoon of mustard powder
- ½ tablespoon of soy sauce
- 1 tablespoon of fresh bleu cheese, crumbled
- 8 medium-sized cherry tomatoes, sliced in half
- 1 cup of fresh arugula, rinsed and patted dry

Directions:
1. 1 Preparing the Ingredients. In a small mixing bowl, combine the soy sauce and onion powder; stir with a fork until thoroughly combined.
2. Lay the raw steak strips in the soy-mustard mixture, and fully immerse each piece to marinate.
3. Set the Instant Crisp Air Fryer to 320 degrees for 10 minutes.
4. Arrange the soy-mustard marinated steak pieces on a piece of tin foil, flat and not overlapping, and set the tin foil on one side of the Instant Crisp Air Fryer basket. The foil should not take up more than half of the surface.
5. Lay the hoagie-bun halves, crusty-side up and soft-side down, on the other half of the air-fryer. 2 Air Frying. Close air fryer lid.
6. After 10 minutes, the Instant Crisp Air Fryer will shut off; the hoagie buns should be starting to crisp and the steak will have begun to cook.
7. Carefully, flip the hoagie buns so they are now crusty-side down and soft-side up; crumble a layer of the bleu cheese on each hoagie half.
8. With a long spoon, gently stir the marinated steak in the foil to ensure even coverage. Set the Instant Crisp Air Fryer to 360 degrees for 6 minutes.
9. After 6 minutes, when the fryer shuts off, the bleu cheese will be perfectly melted over the toasted bread, and the steak will be juicy on the inside and crispy on the outside.
10. Remove the cheesy hoagie halves first, using tongs, and set on a serving plate; then cover one side with the steak, and top with the cherry-tomato halves and the arugula. Close with the other cheesy hoagie-half, slice into two pieces, and enjoy.

Beef Steaks with Beans

Cooking Time: 10 minutes
Serves: 4

Ingredients:
- 4 beef steaks, trim the fat and cut into strips
- 1 cup green onions, chopped
- 2 cloves garlic, minced
- 1 red bell pepper, seeded and thinly sliced
- 1 can tomatoes, crushed
- 1 can cannellini beans
- 3/4 cup beef broth
- 1/4 teaspoon dried basil
- 1/2 teaspoon cayenne pepper
- 1/2 teaspoon sea salt
- 1/4 teaspoon ground black pepper, or to taste

Directions:
1. 1 Preparing the Ingredients. Add the steaks, green onions and garlic to the Instant Crisp Air Fryer basket.
2. 2 Air Frying. Close air fryer lid. Cook at 390 degrees F for 10 minutes, working in batches.
3. Stir in the remaining ingredients and cook for an additional 5 minutes.

Air Fryer Beef Steak

Cooking Time: 15 minutes
Serves: 4

Ingredients:
- 1 tbsp. olive oil
- Pepper and salt
- 2 pounds of ribeye steak

Directions:
1. 1 Preparing the Ingredients. Season meat on both sides with pepper and salt.
2. Rub all sides of meat with olive oil.
3. Preheat Instant Crisp Air Fryer to 356 degrees and spritz with olive oil.
4. 2 Air Frying. Close air fryer lid. Set temperature to 356°F, and set time to 7 minutes. Cook steak 7 minutes. Flip and cook an additional 6 minutes.
5. Let meat sit 2-5 minutes to rest. Slice and serve with salad.

Mushroom Meatloaf

Cooking Time: 25 minutes
Serves: 4

Ingredients:
- 14-ounce lean ground beef
- 1 chorizo sausage, chopped finely
- 1 small onion, chopped
- 1 garlic clove, minced
- 2 tablespoons fresh cilantro, chopped
- 3 tablespoons breadcrumbs
- 1 egg
- Salt and freshly ground black pepper, to taste
- 2 tablespoons fresh mushrooms, sliced thinly
- 3 tablespoons olive oil

Directions:
1. 1 Preparing the Ingredients. Preheat the Instant Crisp Air Fryer to 390 degrees F.
2. In a large bowl, add all ingredients except mushrooms and mix till well combined.
3. In a baking pan, place the beef mixture.
4. With the back of spatula, smooth the surface.
5. Top with mushroom slices and gently, press into the meatloaf.
6. Drizzle with oil evenly.
7. 2 Air Frying. Arrange the pan in the Instant Crisp Air Fryer basket, close air fryer lid and cook for about 25 minutes.
8. Cut the meatloaf in desires size wedges and serve.

Beef and Broccoli

Cooking Time: 12 minutes
Serves: 4

Ingredients
- 1 minced garlic clove
- 1 sliced ginger root
- 1 tbsp. olive oil
- 1 tsp. almond flour
- 1 tsp. sweetener of choice
- 1 tsp. low-sodium soy sauce
- 1/3 C. sherry
- 2 tsp. sesame oil
- 1/3 C. oyster sauce
- 1 pounds of broccoli
- ¾ pound round steak

Directions:
1. 1 Preparing the Ingredients. Remove stems from broccoli and slice into florets. Slice steak into thin strips.
2. Combine sweetener, soy sauce, sherry, almond flour, sesame oil, and oyster sauce together, stirring till sweetener dissolves.
3. Put strips of steak into the mixture and allow to marinate 45 minutes to 2 hours.
4. Add broccoli and marinated steak to Instant Crisp Air Fryer. Place garlic, ginger, and olive oil on top.
5. 2 Air Frying. Close air fryer lid. Set temperature to 400°F, and set time to 12 minutes. Cook 12 minutes at 400 degrees. Serve with cauliflower rice!

Air Fryer Beef Fajitas

Cooking Time: 20 minutes
Serves: 6

Ingredients:
- Beef:
- 1/8 C. carne asada seasoning
- 2 pounds beef flap meat
- Diet 7-Up
- Fajita veggies:
- 1 tsp. chili powder
- 1-2 tsp. pepper
- 1-2 tsp. salt
- 2 bell peppers, your choice of color
- 1 onion

Directions:
1. 1 Preparing the Ingredients. Slice flap meat into manageable pieces and place into a bowl. Season meat with carne seasoning and pour diet soda over meat. Cover and chill overnight.
2. Ensure your Instant Crisp Air Fryer is preheated to 380 degrees.
3. Place a parchment liner into the Instant Crisp Air Fryer basket and spray with olive oil. Place beef in layers into the basket.
4. Cook 8-10 minutes, making sure to flip halfway through. Remove and set to the side.
5. Slice up veggies and spray Instant Crisp Air Fryer basket. Add veggies to the fryer and spray with olive oil.
6. 2 Air Frying. Close air fryer lid. Set temperature to 400°F, and set time to 10 minutes. Cook 10 minutes at 400 degrees, shaking 1-2 times during cooking process.
7. Serve meat and veggies on wheat tortillas and top with favorite keto fillings!

SNACKS AND APPETIZER

Brussels Sprouts

Cooking Time: 15 minutes
Serves: 4

Ingredients:
- Brussels sprouts – 1 pound, trimmed and halved
- Salt and black pepper to taste
- Olive oil – 6 tsps.
- Thyme – ½ tsp. chopped
- Mayonnaise – ½ cup
- Roasted garlic – 2 tbsps. crushed

Directions:
1. Mix Brussels sprouts with oil, salt and pepper in the air fryer basket and toss well. Cook them at 390F for 15 minutes. Meanwhile, in a bowl, mix mayo, thyme, and garlic and whisk well. Divide Brussels sprouts on plates, drizzle garlic sauce all over and serve.

Creamy Potato

Cooking Time: 1 hour 20 minutes
Serves: 2

Ingredients:
- Big potato – 1
- Bacon strips – 2, cooked and chopped
- Olive oil – 1 tsp.
- Cheddar cheese – 1/3 cup, shredded
- Green onions – 1 tbsp. chopped
- Salt and black pepper to taste
- Butter – 1 tbsp.
- Heavy cream – 2 tbsps.

Directions:
1. Rub potato with oil, season with salt and pepper. Place in the preheated air fryer and cook at 400F for 30 minutes. Flip potato, and cook for 30 minutes more. Transfer to a cutting board. Cool and slice in half lengthwise and scoop pulp in a bowl. Add salt, pepper, green onions, heavy cream, butter, cheese, and bacon. Stir well and stuff potato skins with this mix. Return potato to the air fryer and cook them at 400F for 20 minutes. Divide among plates and serve.

Green Beans

Cooking Time: 25 minutes
Serves: 4

Ingredients:
- Green beans – 1 ½ pounds, trimmed and steamed for 2 minutes
- Salt and black pepper to taste
- Shallots – ½ pound, chopped
- Almonds – ¼ cup, toasted
- Olive oil – 2 tbsps.

Directions:
1. Mix green beans with oil, almonds, shallots, salt, and pepper in the air fryer basket. Toss well and cook at 400F for 25 minutes. Divide among plates and serve.

Parmesan Mushrooms

Cooking Time: 15 minutes
Serves: 3

Ingredients:
- Button mushroom caps – 9
- Cream cracker slices – 3, crumbled
- Egg white – 1
- Parmesan – 2 tbsps. grated
- Italian seasoning – 1 tsp.
- Salt and black pepper
- Butter – 1 tbsp. melted

Directions:
1. Mix crackers with butter, Parmesan, salt, pepper, seasoning, and egg white. Stir well and stuff mushrooms with this mix. Arrange mushrooms in the air fryer basket and cook them at 360F for 15 minutes. Divide among plates and serve.

Air Fried Eggplant

Cooking Time: 10 minutes
Serves: 4

Ingredients:
- Baby eggplants – 8, scooped in the center and pulp reserved
- Salt and black pepper to taste
- A pinch of oregano, dried
- Green bell pepper – 1, chopped
- Tomato paste – 1 tbsp.
- Coriander – 1 bunch, chopped
- Garlic powder – ½ tsp.
- Olive oil – 1 tbsp.
- Yellow onion – 1, chopped
- Tomato – 1, chopped

Directions:
1. Heat oil in a pan and add the onion. Stir-fry for 1 minute. Add tomato, coriander, garlic powder, tomato paste, green bell pepper, oregano, eggplant pulp, salt, and pepper. Stir-fry for 2 minutes more. Remove from heat and cool. Stuff eggplants with this mix; place them in the air fryer's basket. Cook at 360F for 8 minutes. Divide eggplants between plates and serve.

Wrapped in Prosciutto Asparagus with Been Dip

Cooking Time: 10 minutes
Serves: 6

Ingredients:
- 1 lb Asparagus, stalks trimmed
- 10 oz Prosciutto, thinly sliced
- For the Dip:
- 1 cup canned white beans
- 1 medium onion, diced
- 2 cloves of garlic, minced
- 2 medium jalapeños, chopped
- 1 cup crushed Tomatoes
- 1 cup vegetable broth
- 1 ½ tbsp olive oil
- 1 tsp paprika
- ¾ tsp sea salt
- ½ tsp chili powder

Directions:
1. Open the cooker and add the white beans, onion, jalapeños, garlic, tomatoes, broth, oil, paprika, chili powder, and salt.
2. Close the lid, secure the pressure valve, and select Pressure mode on High for 8 minutes. Press Start.
3. Once the timer has ended, do a quick pressure release, and open the pot.
4. Transfer the ingredients to a food processor, and blend until creamy and smooth. Set aside. Wrap each asparagus with a slice of prosciutto from top to bottom.
5. Grease the crisp basket with cooking spray, and add in the wrapped asparagus. Close the crisping lid, select Air Fry mode at 370 F and set the time to 8 minutes. Press Start. At the 4-minute mark, turn the bombs. Serve.

Ground Beef & Cabbage Dumplings

Cooking Time: 12 minutes
Serves: 8

Ingredients:
- 8 ounces ground beef
- ½ cup grated cabbage
- 1 carrot, grated
- 1 large egg, beaten
- 1 garlic clove, minced
- 2 tbsp coconut aminos
- ½ tbsp melted ghee
- ½ tbsp ginger powder
- ½ tsp salt
- ½ tsp freshly ground black pepper
- 20 wonton wrappers
- 2 tbsp olive oil

Directions:
1. Close crisping lid. Preheat your cooker by choosing Air Fry at 390 F for 5 minutes.
2. In a large bowl, mix beef, cabbage, carrot, egg, garlic, coconut aminos, ghee, ginger, salt, and pepper. Put wonton wrappers on a clean flat surface and spoon 1 tbsp of the beef mixture into the middle of each wrapper. Run the edges of the wrapper with a little water; fold the wrapper to cover the filling into a semi-circle shape and pinch the edges to seal. Brush the dumplings with olive oil.
3. Lay the dumplings in the preheated basket, choose Air Fry, set the temperature to 390 F, and set the time to 12 minutes. Choose Start.
4. At the 6-minute mark, open the lid, pull out the basket and shake the dumplings. Return the basket to the pot and close the lid to continue frying until the dumplings are crispy to your desire.

Paprika Crispy Wings

Cooking Time: 20 minutes
Serves: 8

Ingredients:
- ½ cup water
- ½ cup sriracha sauce
- 2 tbsp butter, melted
- 1 tbsp lemon juice
- 8 chicken wings
- ½ tsp hot paprika
- Cooking spray

Directions:
1. Mix the water, sriracha, butter and lemon juice in the pot. In the Cook & Crisp basket, put the wings, and then the basket into the pot. Seal the pressure lid.
2. Choose Pressure, set to High, set the timer at 5 minutes, and choose Start.
3. When the timer is done reading, perform a quick pressure release, and carefully open the lid.
4. Pour the paprika all over the chicken and oil with cooking spray. Cover the crisping lid. Choose Air Fry, set the temperature to 375 F, and the timer to 15 minutes. Choose Start to commence frying.
5. After half the Cooking Time, open the crisping lid, shake the wings. Oil the chicken again with cooking spray and return the basket to the pot. Close the lid and continue cooking until the wingettes are crispy.

Cheese & Bacon Filled Sweet Potatoes

Cooking Time: 30 minutes
Serves: 4

Ingredients:
- 12 ounces sweet potatoes
- 1 tsp melted butter
- ¼ cup shredded Monterey Jack cheese
- ¼ cup buttermilk
- 2 slices bacon, cooked and crumbled
- 1 tbsp chopped scallions
- Salt to taste

Directions:
1. Close crisping lid. Preheat your cooker by choosing Air Fry at 390 F for 5 minutes.
2. Toss the sweet potatoes with the melted butter until evenly coated.
3. Add to the Cook & Crisp basket. Close the lid, choose Air Fry, set the temperature to 345 F, and set the time to 30 minutes. Press Start.
4. After 15 minutes, open the lid, pull out the basket and shake the potatoes.
5. At the 15-minute mark, check the potatoes to see if they're crisped to your liking. In a bowl, mix cheese, buttermilk, bacon, and scallions, season with salt and set aside.
6. Take out the potatoes from the basket and halve the potatoes lengthways. Top with the bacon-cheese filling and serve.

Cheesy Bombs in Bacon

Cooking Time: 10 minutes Serves: 8

Ingredients:
- 8 Bacon Slices, cut in half
- 16 oz Mozzarella Cheese, cut into 8 pieces
- 3 tbsp Butter, melted

Directions:
1. Wrap each cheese string with a slice of bacon and secure the ends with toothpicks. Set aside.
2. Grease the crisp basket with the melted butter and add in the bombs. Close the crisping lid, select Air Fry mode, and set the temperature to 370 F and set the time to 10 minutes.
3. At the 5-minute mark, turn the bombs. When ready, remove to a paper-lined plate to drain the excess oil. Serve on a platter with toothpicks.

Goddess Tomato-Basil Dip

Cooking Time: 13 minutes Serves: 6

Ingredients:
- 1 cup chopped Tomatoes
- ¼ cup chopped Basil
- 10 oz shredded Parmesan Cheese
- 10 oz Cream Cheese
- ½ cup Heavy Cream
- 1 cup Water

Directions:
1. Open the cooker and pour in the tomatoes, basil, heavy cream, cream cheese, and water. Close the lid, secure the pressure valve, and select Pressure for 3 minutes at High. Press Start.
2. Once the timer has ended, do a natural pressure release for 10 minutes. Stir the mixture with a spoon while mashing the tomatoes with the back of the spoon. Add the Parmesan cheese and Close the crisping lid. Select Bake mode, set the temperature to 370 F and the time to 3 minutes. Serve with chips.

Nutty Asparagus

Cooking Time: 11 minutes
Serves: 4

Ingredients:
- 1 ½ lb Asparagus, ends trimmed
- Salt and Pepper, to taste
- 1 cup Water
- 1 tbsp butter
- ½ cup chopped Pine Nuts
- 1 tbsp Olive Oil to garnish

Directions:
1. Open the cooker, pour the water in, and fit the reversible rack at the bottom.
2. Place the asparagus on the rack, close the crisping lid, select Air Fry mode, and set the time to 8 minutes on 380 F. Press Start.
3. At the 4-minute mark, carefully turn the asparagus over.
4. When ready, remove to a plate, sprinkle with salt and pepper, and set aside.
5. Select Sear/Sauté on your cooker, set to Medium and melt the butter.
6. Add the pine nuts and cook for 2-3 minutes until golden. Scatter over the asparagus the pine nuts, and drizzle olive oil.

Brazilian Snack Pao de Queijo

Cooking Time: 20 minutes
Serves: 4

Ingredients:
- 2 cups All-purpose flour
- 1 cup Milk
- A pinch of salt
- 2 Eggs, cracked into a bowl
- 2 cups grated Parmesan Cheese
- ½ cup Olive Oil

Directions:
1. Grease the crisp basket with cooking spray and set aside.
2. Put the cooker on Medium and select Sear/Sauté mode.
3. Add the milk, oil, and salt, and let boil. Add the flour and mix it vigorously with a spoon.
4. Let the mixture cool. Once cooled, use a hand mixer to mix the dough well, and add the eggs and cheese while still mixing. The dough should be thick and sticky.
5. Use your hands to make 14 balls out of the mixture, and put them in the greased basket. Put the basket in the pot and close the crisping lid.
6. Select Air Fry, set the temperature to 380 F and set the timer to 15 minutes.
7. At the 7-minute mark, shake the balls. Serve with lemon aioli, garlic mayo or ketchup.

Tomato Bacon Cheeseburger Dip

Cooking Time: 5 minutes
Serves: 10

Ingredients:
- ½ cup chopped Tomatoes
- 10 oz shredded Monterey Jack Cheese
- 10 oz Cream Cheese
- 10 Bacon Slices, chopped roughly
- 1 cup Water

Directions:
1. Turn on the cooker and select Air Fry mode. Set the temperature to 370 F and the time to 8 minutes.
2. Add the bacon pieces and close the crisping lid. Press Start.
3. When ready, open the lid and add the water, cream cheese, and tomatoes. Do Not Stir.
4. Close the lid, secure the pressure valve, and select Pressure mode on High for 5 minutes. Press Start.
5. Once the timer has ended, do a quick pressure release, and open the lid.
6. Stir in the cheddar cheese and mix to combine. Serve with a side of chips.

Cheddar Chicken Dip

Cooking Time: 1 hour 15 minutes
Serves: 6

Ingredients:
- 1 lb Chicken Breast
- ½ cup Breadcrumbs
- 10 oz Cheddar Cheese
- ½ cup Sour Cream
- 10 oz Cream Cheese
- ½ cup Water

Directions:
1. Open the cooker and add the chicken, water, and cream cheese.
2. Close the lid, secure the pressure valve, and select Pressure mode on High for 10 minutes. Press Start.
3. Once the timer has ended, do a quick pressure release, and open the pot.
4. Add the cheddar cheese and shred the chicken with two forks. Sprinkle with breadcrumbs, and close the crisping lid. Select Bake, set the temperature to 380 F and the timer to 3 minutes.
5. Serve warm with veggie bites.

DESSERTS

Chocolate Chip Cookie

Cooking Time: 9 minutes
Serves: 4

Ingredients:
- Softened butter – 3 tbsps.
- Erythritol – ¼ cup plus 1 tbsp. powdered
- Egg yolk – 1
- Almond flour – ½ cup
- Ground white chocolate – 2 tbsps. no sugar added
- Baking soda – ¼ tsp.
- Vanilla – ½ tsp.
- Chocolate chips – ¾ cup, no sugar added

Directions:
1. In a medium bowl, beat the butter and erythritol together until fluffy. Stir in egg yolk. Add the vanilla, baking soda, white chocolate, and flour. Mix well. Stir in the chocolate chips. Line a baking pan with the parchment paper. Spray the parchment paper with nonstick baking spray. Spread the batter into the prepared pan, leaving a ½-inch border on all sides. Bake at 300F for 9 minutes or until cookie is lightly brown and just barely set. Remove the pan from the air fryer and let cook for 10 minutes. Remove the cookie from the pan, remove the parchment paper and let cool on a wire rack.

Marble Cake

Cooking Time: 17 minutes
Serves: 6

Ingredients:
- Erythritol - 7 tbsps. powdered
- Almond flour – ½ cup
- Eggs – 4, whisked
- Baking powder – 1 tsp.
- Cocoa powder – 5 tsps.
- Butter – 2/3 cup, melted
- Lime juice – ½ tsp.

Directions:
1. Preheat the air fryer to 356F. Mix 3 tbsp. of melted butter with the cocoa powder to form a paste. Add the erythritol to the remaining butter and mix well. Stir in the eggs, almond flour, and baking powder and mix until smooth. Pour in the lime and stir. Place a greased baking pan into the air fryer and allow to heat for a minute. Pour some of the batter into the hot pan then add a layer of the chocolate mixture, then the batter, chocolate and lastly top with batter. Use a skewer to create a swirl. Place in the air fryer and bake for 17 minutes.

Chocolate Cake

Cooking Time: 25 minutes Serves: 6

Ingredients:
- Eggs – 3
- Sour cream – ½ cup
- Almond flour – 1 cup
- Erythritol – 2/3 cup, powdered
- Butter – 1 stick, room temperature
- Cocoa powder – 1/3 cup
- Baking powder – 1 tsp.
- Baking soda – ½ tsp.
- Vanilla – 2 tsps.

Directions:
1. Preheat air fryer to 320F. Mix the wet ingredients in a bowl and dry ingredients in another. Gradually pour the dry mixture into the wet. Lightly mix. Place in the air fryer basket. Cook for 25 minutes. Check if the cake is done, if not then cook for another 5 more minutes. Cool on a wire rack.

Lemon Tarts

Cooking Time: 15 minutes
Serves: 4

Ingredients:
- Butter – ½ cup
- Almond flour – ½ pound
- Erythritol – 3 tbsps. powdered
- Lemon – 1 large (juice and zest)
- Lemon curd – 2 tbsps.
- Nutmeg – 1 pinch

Directions:
1. In a bowl, combine erythritol, almond flour, and butter. Mix until looks like breadcrumbs. Then add lemon zest and juice, and cinnamon and mix again. If needed, add 2 tbsps. of water to make a soft dough. Sprinkle pastry tins with almond flour. Add dough and top with lemon curd. Preheat the air fryer to 360F and cook mini lemon tarts for 15 minutes or until ready. Serve.

Coconut Cookies

Cooking Time: 12 minutes
Serves: 10

Ingredients:
- Egg – 1
- Dried coconut – 3 tbsps.
- Butter – 3 oz.
- Erythritol – 2 oz. powdered
- Vanilla extract – 1 tsp.
- Chocolate – 2 oz. no sugar added
- Almond flour – 5 oz.

Directions:
1. In a bowl, beat butter and erythritol until fluffy. Add one egg, vanilla extract and stir to combine. Crush the chocolate into small pieces. Add them to the mixture. Roll small balls with hands. Roll these balls in the dried coconut. Place balls on the baking sheet. Preheat the air fryer to 370F. Bake coconut balls for 8 minutes. Shake once. Lower temperature to 280 to 300F and cook for 4 minutes more. Serve.

Vanilla Cream Cheese Filled Tart

Cooking Time: 20 minutes   Serves: 4

Ingredients:
- 1 frozen piecrust, thawed
- 2 ½ cups fresh raspberries, divided
- 1 tbsp arrowroot starch
- ¼ cup sugar
- ¼ tsp grated lemon zest
- 1 tsp vanilla extract
- 8 ounces cream cheese, at room temperature
- ½ cup confectioners' sugar
- ¼ cup heavy (whipping) cream
- 1 tsp freshly squeezed lemon juice
- Cream Filling

Directions:
1. Roll out the pie crust and fit into a tart pan. Prick all over the bottom of the dough. Place the reversible rack in the pot and put the tart pan on top. Close the crisping lid, choose Bake; adjust the temperature to 250 F and the Cooking Time to 15 minutes. Press Start. Set the crust aside to cool.
2. Fetch out 1 cup of berries into the inner pot. In a bowl, whisk arrowroot starch and 2 tbsps water until mixed. Pour the slurry on the raspberries along with sugar, lemon zest, and lemon juice. Mix. Seal the pressure lid, choose Pressure; adjust the pressure to High and the Cooking Time to 2 minutes. Press Start.
3. Once done cooking, perform a quick pressure release and carefully open the lid. Add the remaining 1½ cups of raspberries, stirring to coat with the cooked mixture. Then, allow cooling. In a bowl and with a hand mixer, whisk the vanilla extract and cream cheese until evenly combined and smooth.
4. Mix in confectioners' sugar and whisk again until the sugar has fully incorporated and the mixture is light and smooth. With clean whisks and in another bowl, beat the heavy cream until soft peaks form. Fold the heavy cream into the vanilla mixture. Spoon the cream filling into the piecrust and scatter the remaining raspberries on the cream. Chill for 30 minutes before serving.

Hot Lava Cake

Cooking Time: 29 minutes
Serves: 8

Ingredients:
- 1 cup Butter
- 4 tbsp Milk
- 4 tsp Vanilla Extract
- 1 ½ cups Chocolate Chips
- 1 ½ cups Sugar
- Powdered sugar to garnish
- 7 tbsp All-purpose Flour
- 5 Eggs
- 1 cup Water

Directions:
1. Grease the cake pan with cooking spray and set aside. Open the cooker, fit the reversible rack at the bottom of it, and pour in the water.
2. In a medium heatproof bowl, add the butter and chocolate and melt them in the microwave for about 2 minutes. Remove it from the microwave. Add sugar and stir well. Add the eggs, milk, and vanilla extract and stir again. Finally, add the flour and stir until smooth. Pour the batter into the greased cake pan and use the spatula to level it.
3. Place the pan on the trivet in the pot, close the lid, secure the pressure valve, select Pressure on High for 15 minutes. Press Start. Once the timer has gone off, do a natural pressure release for 10 minutes.
4. Remove the pan to a flat surface. Put a plate over the pan and flip the cake over into the plate. Pour the powdered sugar in a fine sieve and sift it over the cake. Use a knife to cut the cake into 8 slices and serve immediately (while warm).

Christmas Chocolate Cheesecake

Cooking Time: 25 minutes + 6 hours for cooling
Serves: 8

Ingredients:
- Crust:
- 1 cup Graham Crackers Crumbs
- 1 tbsp Sugar
- 3 tbsp Cocoa Powder
- 3 tbsp Butter, melted

Filling:
- 2 Eggs, room temperature, cracked
- 2 Egg Yolks, room temperature, cracked
- 20 oz Cream Cheese, room temperature
- ½ cup Granulated Sugar
- ½ cup Cocoa Powder
- 1 cup Heavy Cream
- ½ cup Sour Cream
- 2 tsp Vanilla Extract
- 8 oz Baking Chocolate, melted

Directions:
1. Line a cake pan with parchment paper.
2. In a mixing bowl, add the graham crackers crumbs, cocoa powder, and sugar. Mix evenly then add the melted butter and mix again until well incorporated.
3. Spoon the mixture into the pan and tap it to firm using the spoon. Set aside.
4. Using an electric mixer, beat the cream cheese and cocoa powder. While still mixing, add the eggs and egg yolks. Once combined and still mixing, add the sour cream, melted chocolate, heavy cream, and vanilla extract. Scrape the sides of the bowl as you mix. Once well combined, turn off the electric mixer, and spoon the filling mixture onto the crust in the springform pan. Use the spatula to smoothen it out. Fit A rack in the cooker and pour in 2 cups of water.
5. Cover the pan with foil and place on the reversible rack. Close the lid, select pressure mode on High pressure for 25 minutes. Press Start.
6. Once the timer has stopped, do a natural pressure release for 10 minutes, then a quick pressure release to let out the remaining steam. With napkins in both hands, hold the trivet's sling and lift it out with the spring form pan. Let the cake sit for an hour to cool and then refrigerate for 5 hours. Slice the cake to serve.

Wonderful Vanilla Pudding with Berries

Cooking Time: 18 minutes + 6h for refrigeration
Serves: 4

Ingredients:
- 1 cup Heavy Cream
- 4 Egg Yolks
- 4 tbsp Water + 1 ½ cups Water
- ½ cup Milk
- 1 tsp Vanilla
- ½ cup Sugar
- 4 Raspberries
- 4 Blueberries

Directions:
1. Turn on your cooker and select Sear/Sauté mode on Medium. Add four tbsps for water and the sugar. Stir it constantly until it dissolves. Press Stop. Add milk, heavy cream, and vanilla. Stir it with a whisk until evenly combined.
2. Crack the eggs into a bowl and add a tbsp of the cream mixture. Whisk it and then very slowly add the remaining cream mixture while whisking.
3. Fit the reversible rack at the bottom of the pot, and pour one and a half cup of water in it. Pour the mixture into four ramekins and place them on the rack.
4. Close the lid of the pot, secure the pressure valve, and select Pressure mode on High Pressure for 4 minutes. Press Start.
5. Once the timer has gone off, do a quick pressure release, and open the lid.
6. With a napkin in hand, carefully remove the ramekins onto a flat surface. Let them cool for about 15 minutes and then refrigerate them for 6 hours.
7. After 6 hours, remove them from the refrigerator and garnish them with the raspberries and blueberries.

Strawberry Ricotta Cheesecake

Cooking Time: 25 minutes
Serves: 6

Ingredients:
- 10 oz Cream Cheese
- ¼ cup Sugar
- ½ cup Ricotta Cheese
- One Lemon, zested and juiced
- 2 Eggs, cracked into a bowl
- 1 tsp Lemon Extract
- 3 tbsp Sour Cream
- 1 ½ cups Water
- 10 Strawberries, halved to decorate

Directions:
1. In the electric mixer, add the cream cheese, quarter cup of sugar, ricotta cheese, lemon zest, lemon juice, and lemon extract. Turn on the mixer and mix the ingredients until a smooth consistency is formed. Adjust the sweet taste to liking with more sugar.
2. Reduce the speed of the mixer and add the eggs. Fold it in at low speed until it is fully incorporated. Make sure not to fold the eggs in high speed to prevent a cracker crust. Grease the spring form pan with cooking spray and use a spatula to spoon the mixture into the pan. Level the top with the spatula and cover it with foil.
3. Open the cooker, fit in the reversible rack, and pour in the water. Place the cake pan on the rack. Close the lid, secure the pressure valve, and select Pressure mode on High pressure for 15 minutes. Press Start.
4. Meanwhile, mix the sour cream and one tbsp of sugar. Set aside.
5. Once the timer has gone off, do a natural pressure release for 10 minutes, then a quick pressure release to let out any extra steam, and open the lid.
6. Remove the rack with pan, place the spring form pan on a flat surface, and open it. Use a spatula to spread the sour cream mixture on the warm cake. Refrigerate the cake for 8 hours. Top with strawberries; slice it into 6 pieces and serve while firming.

www.ingramcontent.com/pod-product-compliance
Lightning Source LLC
Chambersburg PA
CBHW081119080526
44587CB00021B/3672